A Supernatural Primer
for the Millions

Books by Susy Smith

ESP

WORLD OF THE STRANGE

THE MEDIUMSHIP OF MRS. LEONARD

THE ENIGMA OF OUT-OF-BODY TRAVEL

ESP FOR THE MILLIONS

A SUPERNATURAL PRIMER FOR THE MILLIONS

Books Edited by Susy Smith

HUMAN PERSONALITY AND ITS SURVIVAL OF BODILY DEATH

A SUPERNATURAL PRIMER
FOR THE MILLIONS

by Susy Smith

PSYCHIC SELF-IMPROVEMENT SERIES

SHERBOURNE PRESS, INC.   Los Angeles, Calif. 90035

CONTENTS

For Jocelyn Davidson
OF VANCOUVER, BRITISH COLUMBIA

The kind of friend
who deserves to have
a book dedicated to him

CHAPTER ONE

Introduction

The supernatural is always with us. Even though we tend to laugh them off in this modern world, unexplainable mysteries occur all the time. And they always have. All through history, there have been records, for instance, of predictions which came true: the Oracles of Delphi in Ancient Greece were the Huntley-Brinkley of their day, and their truthful soothsaying won them immortal fame. Ghosts, poltergeists, and haunted houses continually crop up in the news, and the offered explanations that they are mere imagination, or hallucinations, or trickery aren't really convincing. Sea monsters, unidentified flying objects from outer space, these may be more fiction than fact; but there are many persons, otherwise quite sane and normal, to swear that they have seen these very phenomena.

Those who pick up this book to read are, hopefully, open-minded. Many people, however, claim to have no interest in the supernatural. Perhaps that is all right for them, but I think they are closing their eyes to half the fun of life. These individuals don't believe in or even consider the possible reality of anything which is not within their ordinary routine. They make no effort to have new experiences because they are afraid it will disturb their settled ways of thinking. Such people have a tendency to dismiss as "just a bunch of kooks" those of us who are involved with the more unusual areas of life.

But many who have seen flying saucers and ghosts and materializations and apports were not kooks, were not unsettled or neurotic. They were just ordinary everyday individuals going about their routine affairs until suddenly they were confronted with facts which did not make any sense at all. Most of them have retained their reason, nonetheless. It is true that one can become unsettled if he accepts everything "far out" without critical appraisal, and if he gullibly bases his life on a desire for further magical experiences rather than a sensible evaluation of what he has seen and undergone.

In direct contrast with those who go a bit barmy, there are others who devote themselves to observing and studying supernormal manifestations in an objective manner. These people are called psychical researchers, or parapsychologists. They investigate out-of-the-way phenomena, never admitting that anything has been proved and hardly ever confessing to having seen any convincing evidence. Yet even these hard-headed researchers recognize that there is a small percentage of fact in all the fiction. If 90 per cent of all alleged spirit communication, Unidentified Flying Objects, psychic healings, and ghosts were fraud or misapprehension—and I'm inclined to doubt that the percentage is nearly so high—the remaining 10 per cent which cannot possibly be explained by normal means is so fascinating that one feels it has to be confronted and understood. Those who once get hooked on psychical research want to spend the rest of their lives trying to find the answers to its mysteries.

For the past ten years I've worked continually among those interested in the study of the supernormal and have become aware of the value of human testimony. I don't believe all those who claim they've seen strange and unexplainable phenomena are necessarily suffering from delusions or hallucinations. If someone claims to have seen something which is impossible, perhaps it is what we consider "impossible" that is at fault and not the poor observation of the individual involved. Since my research into these subjects began, I have seen things which cannot be given satisfactory or "normal" explanations. Yet, when I witnessed these things, I was as rational as I ever was in my life. So if another person declares he has seen or experienced the same thing, who am I to think him some kind of a nut?

Well, you get the idea. This book will deal with subjects which are highly curious and controversial, and perhaps a bit spooky. As we delve into the records of the supernormal we will accept the testimony of the ages, and the testimony of the present. Some of what we will discuss may be fable, some may be fraud; but there is also a great deal that is probably fact. So let us keep our wits about us and try to separate the unreal from the real, the false from the true. It won't be easy. But why should it be? Who wants all the answers handed to him on a platter? Where's the challenge in that?

CHAPTER TWO

Mythical Monsters

Dragons play a large role in our childhood fantasies, and St. George is one of our heroes as he slays the beast and saves the beautiful maiden from its gory clutches. Dragons are large and scaly and breathe fire, but we know they aren't real and so we tolerate them in fairly friendly fashion.

Almost everybody knows about centaurs, too, because of our heritage from Greek mythology. They were the creatures with men's heads, trunks, and arms and the bodies and legs of horses. Pictures or statutes of centaurs show a combination of noble-browed men with glistening muscles and white stallions of grace and dignity. Centaurs were so lovely I almost wish they were real.

But not all mythical monsters are so photogenic. Cerberus, the three-headed dog who guarded the mythological gates of Hades, must have been rather startling, to say the least. Especially if all three heads were snarling at once. And the Minotaur was a thoroughly unpleasant character. This grotesque dominator of the Greek Isle of Crete was described in two different ways, neither of

13

them very appealing. He either had the body of a man and the head of a bull, or the head of a man and the body of a bull. Whichever way he was constructed, his habits were atrocious. He required annually to be fed seven handsome youths and seven beautiful maidens of Athens. Fortunately, the Minotaur was killed by Theseus before he decimated the youth of the Greek nation.

Norse mythology had its bovine element, too. A cow of outsized proportions called Adhumbla provided the vast amount of milk necessary to build the muscles of the giant Ymir, the father of all the giants of the Northland. And America has its own famous magic mythical monster in Babe—the gigantic blue ox belonging to Paul Bunyan —a creature so large that her footprints account for the many lakes of Minnesota.

Most of the current legends don't involve fantastic animals or animal-man combinations, except for a certain prehistoric type which is fairly prevalent. The susquatch, a large, hairy, man-like animal, or animal-like man, is reported to slink about the woods of Northern California, and werewolves supposedly abound in Scandinavia.

Does the abominable snowman actually leap from mountainous crag to glacial peak in the tallest of all mountains, the Himalayas of India and Tibet? Naturalist Ivan Sanderson makes a pretty good case for the possible existence of such an entity, which, he believes, may very well live secretly in various wilderness expanses and never be revealed. He points out in *Abominable Snowman: Legend Come to Life** that in unpopulated areas we are even today finding varieties of animals not previously known. It was not until 1910 that the second largest land animal

* Philadelphia, Chilton Co., 1961.

in the world, a kind of rhinocerous, was found in Africa. The fabulous okapi is also a newcomer to the ranks of known flora and fauna, and the Congo peacock had to wait until 1936 to be discovered. The kraken, or giant squid, was regarded as a fable for centuries until Professor A. E. Verrill took a small boat and captured one alive off the coast of Newfoundland.

Sanderson also suggests the possibility of men with limited intelligence hiding out somewhere in the vast, partially unexplored world. He ventures that they are no doubt large, smelly chaps with nasty habits, but they are definitely rather human. Since they are also picturesque and fascinating, I rather resent someone like Marlin Perkins coming along and debunking them. Well, actually, I guess I don't really. Perkins is such a nice-looking man, and his stories about nature on television are so fascinating that I guess I'll have to forgive him; but it is rather a shame to have to do away with something as colorful as the abominable snowman.

The snowman, or yeti, to give it its proper name, appeared first in a book written in 1887 by an English mountaineer, Major Lawrence A. Waddell. Information about this elusive creature has remained sketchy and fragmentary ever since. In the fall of 1951 an English explorer named Eric Shipton photographed mysterious tracks on the Menlung glacier in the Mt. Everest region, and his remarkable film appeared to lend documentary evidence to the story. What are said to be yeti scalps have also been discovered in the possession of native Sherpas who live in that region.

But Marlin Perkins, director of the Lincoln Park Zoo in Chicago, and others who accompanied Sir Edmund P. Hillary on the World Book Encyclopedia Scientific Expedition to the Himalayas in 1960–61, debunked the yeti on at least three counts. First, they bought from one native, the wife of a lama, an alleged yeti skin, which they almost immediately identified as the skin of a Tibetan blue bear. Perkins also realized that the naturally superstitious and simple mountain people have mistakenly accounted for the weird sounds which ring out in their long, dark nights; the cries of snow leopards, not yetis.

But what about the photographed yeti tracks? The expedition members also saw them. It was discovered, however, that these were actually fox tracks. No, not some huge mythical fox; just a little anybody kind of fox. But four fox tracks, when melted by sunshine, ran into one large track which looked like a human foot. The investigators started out in the shade tracking the small animal, clearly able to see his pad and claw marks. As the tracks proceeded into the sunlight, they noticed a most curious thing. The broken snow of the four tracks had melted into one large ovoid track, roughly the size of a human footprint. The sun even developed toelike projections on those ovoid depressions as the snow softened more and more. In other words, the trail started out in the shade as fox tracks in the snow, changed in the sun to yeti prints, and then became fox tracks again.

"So here was the answer," Perkins wrote.* "Foxes had made them; perhaps wolves could make them, too, or snow leopards, or mountain sheep, or serows."

Serows are rather uncommon members of the goat-antelope family, and if some mischievous Sherpa a couple of centuries ago had taken a piece of serow hide and sewed

---

* *World Book Encyclopedia Year Book, 1962*, Field Enterprises Educational Corp., Chicago, 1962.

it together into a cap, do you know what it would be called now? A yeti scalp. Yes, sir, Perkins and party exploded the claim about these famous relics just that easily. A scalp allegedly of an abominable snowman, which was said to be 240 years old, was brought to them in Khumjung. It looked like a hairy, pointed, brimless helmet, but it also looked like serow pelt to Perkins. He asked the elders of Khumjung if he might take the scalp back to America and Europe for scientific appraisal, on his word of honor that he would return it within six weeks.

"Permission was granted after we had overcome their objections and agreed to all their conditions," says Perkins. "They insisted as an added precaution that all the worldly possessions of our three head Sherpas be forfeited in the event that the scalp was not returned in six weeks." Specialists at the Chicago Natural History Museum pronounced the yeti scalp to be a man-made artifact from the skin of the Himalayan serow. The evidence was then flown to Paris and London to be examined by other noted scientists. They, too, found the scalp had been fabricated from the skin of the serow.

So what now for the abominable snowman? "We are convinced he is a myth," Perkins says. "But he probably will live on among the Sherpas as the legendary figure he has been for centuries."

Perhaps like the abominable snowman, most other land-based monster stories *are* myths. But what about sea serpents? How in the world can we ever become sure where fact about them ends and fiction begins? Most sea animals are such monstrosities that we wouldn't believe them even now if we didn't have their living, squirming bodies right before us in aquariums everywhere. Stories of

17

sea monsters have been going around as long as there have been men to tell tales of the sea. Surely we can believe these?

The first person to write in any detail about sea serpents was a Swedish archbishop named Olaus Magnus, or Olaus the Great, who published a somewhat fictional history of the Scandinavian nations in the early Sixteenth Century. In it he mentioned the kraken, or giant squid which was taken to be a myth then and for many centuries thereafter, until, as I've already mentioned, somebody caught one and towed it ashore and proved its existence.

Another creature described by Olaus Magnus was an undulating sea serpent 200 feet long and 20 feet around, with a head like a huge snake. The woodcut which accompanied this description showed the serpent attacking a sailing vessel and two lifeboats off the coast of Norway. This picture has been reprinted in dozens of textbooks and encyclopedias since then, but always with the idea that it showed a mythical sea monster.

Some reported sightings, however, make one wonder if perhaps lurking about somewhere in the deep there may not be an actual creature made along a similar pattern. A book by Professor A. C. Oudemans published in 1892 called *The Great Sea Serpent* contains some 200 reports of similar serpents. For instance: On July 6, 1734 a Norwegian priest named Hans Egede sighted off the west coast of Greenland "a very terrible sea monster," which raised itself so high out of the water that its head reached above the top of the ship. The body of the serpent seemed to be covered with a hard skin, and broad flippers extended from either side of it.

Oudemans also says that between August 10 and August

23, 1817 a number of people saw a sea serpent in Massachusetts Bay near the Gloucester Harbor. A Boston committee was appointed to study the reports, most of which agreed that the creature was some 80 to 90 feet in length, with a head like a snake and a jointed body. It was dark brown in color. In all, the committee collected reports from hundreds of people, some of whom claimed to have been within 20 feet of the serpent. After August 23rd the creature was not seen again in the Massachusetts Bay area, but it was reported by two different ships some six weeks later, off Rye Point in Long Island Sound.

In 1848 both the London *Illustrated News* and the *Times* stirred up great interest throughout England with their account of a sighting on August 6th of a sea serpent more than 60 feet in length. It was said to have passed at a speed of some 12 to 15 miles an hour, so close to the *H.M.S. Daedalus,* a British man-of-war cruising in the South Atlantic, that the captain and crew had it in view for about twenty minutes.

Similar tales come from this century as well. A German submarine, the *U-28,* encountered a sea serpent in the early days of World War I. On July 30, 1915, after torpedoing a British steamer, the captain and crew of the sub spotted a sea serpent floundering in the area of the wreckage. They reported it as about 66 feet long, and though they attempted to photograph it they weren't fast enough to get anything but a blur on their picture.

An even more modern sighting occurred on December 30, 1947 when the Grace Lines *S. S. Santa Clara* was 118 miles due east of Cape Lookout, en route from New York to Cartagena. On a clear, calm day, with bright sunshine and perfect visibility, the ship hit a sea serpent which had a head about 5 feet long and a body about 3 feet thick. The third mate saw the snake-like head break the surface of the water some 30 feet off the vessel's starboard bow. He and two other mates reported that the ship apparently had cut this animal in two. The water about the ship was stained blood-red. About 35 feet of the serpent's length was visible to the three witnesses, but since no one on the other side of the vessel saw it, it is not known whether or not it extended in the other direction. The serpent was dark brown in color and had no fins, flippers, or humps.

The Loch Ness monster, the modern world's most prominent sea myth, is historically quite new on the scene, having first been sighted officially in 1933, but its legend goes back much farther than that. Every year brings new eyewitness reports of what it looks like: long and slinky, humped or bumped, feathered or finned. Whenever photographs of it are taken they always seem to be blurred, or the object is too far away to show up clearly. Some people claim to have seen it closely, though. A few have even insisted that it passed over dry land, crossing a nearby road. Scientific expeditions have so far found nothing absolutely convincing, and even a recent search by men armed with a powerful army searchlight to blind and bewilder it has not proved nor disproved the existence of the famous Loch Ness monster.

I hope it never is either proved or disproved. We have too few fantasies in our lives as it is.

CHAPTER THREE

Alchemy

Many scientists who are hard at work today trying to produce living tissue may not be aware that their search is actually old hat. It's been done before—scientists in the Middle Ages also made an effort to synthesize human life.

In our funny way of laughing at the foibles of the past, we think of alchemists as mere wizards with pointed hats and flowing robes, forgetting that they were actually the first chemists. And they had many ideas not too far behind those we hold today. The biggest project in the lives of several alchemists was the construction of an artificial living man. Homunculus is the word for this entity, and whether or not anybody ever actually succeeded in inventing one is a moot question. Paracelsus, a Sixteenth Century alchemist, was convinced that he knew the technique of producing one. His procedures might not stand up to the scrutiny of present-day laboratory technicians, but at least he was trying.

Paracelsus wrote that, in order to make a Homunculus, the "needful spagyric substances" should be taken and shut up in a glass phial and afterwards be placed to digest in horse dung for the space of forty days. If he had only published a list of these spagyric substances, we might be in the man-production business today; and think how popular the horse would be. For Paracelsus assured us that if we followed his techniques, "At the end of this time, there will be something which will begin to move and live in the bottle. This something is a man, but a man who has no body and is transparent. Nevertheless, he exists, and nothing remains but to bring him up—which is not more difficult to do than to make him. You may accomplish it by daily feeding him—during forty weeks, and without extricating him from his dung hill—with the arcanum [elixir] of human blood. At the end of this time you shall have a veritable living child, having every member as well-proportioned as any infant born of a woman. He will only be much smaller than an ordinary child, and his physical education will require more care and attention."

Imagine how progressive a man must have been in the Middle Ages even to conceive of the possibility of making an actual human being. Some alchemists were like that. They reached out in their thinking, living dedicated lives as they attempted to formulate general laws and deduce truths from their research, just as scientists do today. Oh, yes, there were alchemists who were charlatans, but many of them were truly hard-working men, and some of their discoveries are still of value to us today.

It was a woman alchemist, Mary the Jewess, who invented, or discovered, the still; at least, she is the first person to describe one. The double boiler, or *bain marie*, is named for her. This invention, in turn, led to the distillation of alcohol. Paracelsus introduced into medicine the

22

use of opium, compounds of antimony, and mercury. He even worked with ether as an anesthesia.

The great psychoanalyst Carl G. Jung spent years researching alchemy. He did this because he saw a great deal to the subject and believed that some of the best-known alchemists were men with vision far beyond their contemporaries. Perhaps with his thorough grounding in the obtuse terminology of psychoanalysis, Jung was able to understand the writings of the alchemists. Few others have been able to decipher the meaning of their magical and mystical terminology, possibly so written to keep from revealing their secrets.

The dictionary defines alchemy as "the chemistry of the Middle Ages, the chief purposes of which were to turn common metals into gold and to find a method of prolonging life." A more elaborate explanation, from the *Dictionary of Mysticism*, says that alchemy is "The science of decomposing and recomposing things, as well as of changing their essential nature and raising it higher—transmuting them into each other. While chemistry deals with lifeless matter, alchemy employs life as a factor, and deals with higher forces of nature and the conditions of matter under which they operate. In its lowest aspect, it deals with physical substances, but in its highest aspect it teaches the regeneration of the spiritual man, the purification of mind, will, and thought, and the enobling of all the faculties of the human soul."

The means the alchemists hoped to use in transmuting metals was known as "the philosopher's stone," a magical ingredient which they believed would someday be found to change base metals into gold. When dissolved in alcohol this stone would form an Elixir of Life, a medicine which

23

would cure all ills and prolong life, they thought. It was a common belief of the times that the philosopher's stone existed even though nobody knew where to find it.

The misconception came originally from Aristotle, who had started the whole thing by saying that a prime matter existed which was the basis of all substances in the terrestrial world. The interaction of matter and form, he stated, gave rise to the four elements: fire, air, water, and earth. These basic elements, in turn, through their various combinations, produced all material objects. Thus, changes in the proportion of these elements resulted in changes in the form of the prime matter, and so, in theory, any substance could be transmuted into any other substance if the suitable conditions could be found. The trick, of course, was to find the right proportions of the right combinations of elements, stir correctly, time exactly, and presto chango! Gold, or a reasonable facsimile thereof, might emerge.

Because of the fact that alchemists were attempting to produce a substance held in such popular esteem as gold, their work was often underwritten by kings and wealthy nobles in a forerunner of the modern research grant. But when they were unable to perform the necessary hocus pocus, alchemists were liable to lose their lives in their endeavor. And so it took a brave man to devote himself to this.

Such a man was Paracelsus, who would have been outstanding in any age. He is said to have been born in Zurich in 1493 and named Auroelus Philippus Theoprastus Bombast von Hohenheim. He conferred upon himself the *nom de plume* of "Paracelsus" which indicated that he was greater than Celsus, the Roman physician who was the leading medical authority of the Middle Ages. He studied medicine and metallurgy, chemistry and alchemy in the Middle East, and perhaps even in the Far East as he claimed. Then he settled down as a professor of medicine at the University of Basle. There he began his practice of alchemy in earnest, and he also experimented with hypnotism, which he called magnetism. Although his mind was rich and inventive, Paracelsus must have had a difficult disposition. He was so bigoted and egotistical that he could not get along at all with his colleagues and was eventually forced out of his position on the faculty at Basle. If he had not been killed while still in his forties, who knows what great and exciting things we may have heard from him?

Perhaps Paracelsus might even have achieved the success with his Homunculus that another well-known alchemist is said to have had. Albert Magnus is reported to have kept in his laboratory a beautiful woman whom he had actually constructed there. Since he was a devout churchman, his motives have not been questioned, and perhaps it is just as well.

CHAPTER FOUR

Astrology

Astrology's history is as old as man's endeavors. It was studied by the ancient Egyptians, Chaldeans, Assyrians, Hindus, Chinese, and Babylonians. It's the oldest science in existence, according to the claims of astrologers; but there are many others who will give you an argument as to whether or not it *is* a science. Astronomers, for instance.

It may be true that astronomy is an outgrowth of astrology, just as chemistry is an outgrowth of alchemy. Carroll Righter, a well-known present-day astrologer, says in his book *Astrology and You** "Astrology dates back to the earliest archeological research. Man was interested in the effect of the heavenly bodies upon him (which is astrology) long before he became concerned with their relation to one another (which is astronomy)." He says that the rules governing astrology were not something conjured from the minds of the early astrologians but were the result of careful study, checking, and rechecking.

Astrology is defined as the belief in and study of the influence upon human character of cosmic forces emanat-

* Fleet Publishing Corp., 1956.

ing from celestial bodies. Statements in its favor have been made for the record as early as the time of Hippocrates, who lived from 460 to 357 B.C. He required his students to study astrology and was so convinced of its value that he said, "The man who does not understand astrology is to be called fool rather than physician."

A more recent quote is from Sir Isaac Newton, who is said to have recognized the Law of Gravity when an apple dropped on his head. When Lord Halley, discoverer of Halley's Comet, disdainfully said, referring to astrology, "Do you believe in *that?*" Newton replied, "I have studied the subject, sir. You have not."

Present-day astrology enthusiasts include countless movie stars, whose very careers have sometimes hung on astrological consultations. Among those who have admitted an interest in the subject are Adolph Menjou, Joan Collins, Susan Hayward, Lana Turner, Peter Lawford, and Arlene Dahl. It is said that at least 100 of the best-known Hollywood personalities consult astrologians on such matters as what to eat, what to wear and when to make love, as well as when to see their producers and sign contracts.

People who scoff often point out in ridicule such things as the many astrological predictions that the world is coming to an end. They also call attention to the daily horoscopes in every newspaper which give advice for the day in terms so indefinite that they can apply to anyone. These skeptics are quite reluctant to think that the sun, the moon, and the planets care a thing about their personal lives, and they laugh at those who do. Astronomers declaim that not the slightest evidence has been found to justify the belief that the planets can change the course of ordinary human events.

Yet it is extremely difficult for astrologer Dal Lee to fathom the reason orthodox scientists refuse to investigate the claim of legitimate astrology—or so he says. "If celestial angles formed by sun, earth, and moon can move millions of tons of ocean back and forth to produce tides," he writes,* "and if angular patterns formed among major planets can appreciably affect radio broadcasting and reception as proved in the laboratories of the Radio Corporation of America, is it wasteful of time to consider the possibilities that the planets and their varying angles may affect the metabolic processes of the human body? If it is agreed that brain, glands, and nerves condition our thinking, why not search for a connection between cosmic rays and our actions? . . . Astrologers believe that there are natural laws at work influencing our behavior."

Lee believes that it is not the function of astrology to predict the future as much as it is to explain a person's aptitudes and abilities so that they might be made use of to their utmost possibilities. After all, he says, "A man set on the right course, with confidence and understanding, need not worry about his future. He is not interested in isolated events of the future, for he knows he will have the fortitude to face them all and sundry."

Casting a horoscope requires a specialized language and a great deal of technical information. A horoscope is an hour picture or map or chart indicating the positions of the sun, the moon, and seven planets in relation to the earth and to the signs of the zodiac at the hour of a per-

* "Astrology; Facts and Fallacies," *Tomorrow Magazine*, Vol 8, No. 3, Summer, 1960.

son's birth. The signs of the zodiac are Aries, Taurus, Gemini, Cancer, Leo, Virgo, Libra, Scorpio, Sagittarius, Capricorn, Aquarius, and Pisces. Each of them corresponds to approximately 30 days on the calendar.

In preparing the horoscope, the astrologer must first of all know something of the mathematics of astronomy. "His task," Lee says, "is to determine the true horizon of the earth at the exact minute of the native's birth. Both spatial and temporal factors enter the proceedings; he must be sure of his geography (latitude and longitude of the birthplace) and careful in his conversion of clock time to sidereal [stellar] time. This is no simple assignment, what with local time, Greenwich Mean Time, and various divisions of Standard Time zones, and nowadays the added problem of daylight-saving time. Yet the sincere practitioner is painstaking in his operations, for he knows a good interpretation can be delivered only if based on a true hour picture of the heavens."

Astrologer Evangeline Adams says: that "It should be clearly understood that the stars only indicate what will come to pass if intelligence and free will are not used to change the natural course of events. The wise man cooperates with the stars, the fool thinks he rules them."*

Mrs. Adams goes on: "Had Napoleon exercised intelligence and taken the warning of his professional astrologer that he would suffer defeat if he met Wellington at Waterloo, his whole destiny and that of France might have been changed. Had Abraham Lincoln been informed through astrology that he was under accidental and treacherous vibrations, he might have exercised his free will and

* *Astrology, Your Place in the Sun*, New York, Dodd, Mead & Co., 1956.

avoided making himself a target by appearing in so public a place as a theatre the night he was assassinated."

Two people who speak just as dogmatically the other way about astrology are L. Sprague and Catherine C. deCamp, who say in their book *Spirits, Stars and Spells**: "Unquestionably, astrology fails as a science. Its basic assumptions are illusory. A planet does not 'rise' in the night sky. Instead, the earth turns towards the planet. Planets are never really 'in conjunction'; they remain millions of miles apart no matter how close they appear. Aside from very slight changes in light, gravitation, and magnetism, the other planets do not affect the earth at all. The astrologer's vibrations' never make the needle of any instrument quiver. In short, astrology produces results no more reliable than simple guesswork.

"What, then, keeps astrology so much alive? For one thing, its apparatus of fascinating symbols, mysterious charts, and abstruse calculations gives it a scientific appearance, which dazzles many simple souls. Furthermore, astrologers are experts at telling people what they want to hear...."

That's where your author comes into the picture. Astrology always tells me what I want to hear, it seems. I must admit that the statements in the daily horoscopes in the papers or magazines are appalling. And I feel that a subject has to be judged by the front it presents to the public. However, I have also to admit that every description of the character and personality of one in my zodiac sign seems to fit me perfectly. Having been born in the early part of June, I love to read the things about myself listed for Geminis. If they weren't usually so flattering, I

* Canaveral Press, New York, 1966.

31

wouldn't, of course. But who can resist enjoying the information, as I learn it from Carroll Righter, that Geminis have alive, facile minds and are brilliant, alert, and active mentally? Righter says, "You enjoy letting your mind roam the universe and like to study new approaches to all that comes within the purview of your consciousness. Fortunately, you are usually open-minded and it is therefore possible for you to look at a condition exactly as it is.

"As a matter of fact, your greatest quality probably is your quick adaptability which is so rapid that you are immediately able to handle emergencies that could leave others prostrate or bewildered."

I am certain that my deep and abiding interest in psychical research is amply explained by the following: "You like to experiment with and investigate everything which comes into the realm of your vision. . . . Your logical mind is constantly searching for untried and unthought-of horizons."

Not to keep all the goodies for myself, however, I must confess that I've also found the horoscopes of my friends to reveal their character traits in a way which has helped me on more than one occasion to understand their puzzling actions.

So I will leave astrology in limbo with the rest of the mysteries I've discussed so far. If you like it, have fun with it. If you don't, please don't blame me.

CHAPTER FIVE

Witchcraft

During World War II white witches, with their spells and incantations, drew a protective ring about England, and they are sure that they helped maintain its security in the face of bombs and Hitler. So, you see, there are witches after all. They really do exist. Of course, they're all white—or good—witches now. Certainly nobody these days would admit to being an ordinary, unfashionable, old black witch.

The best-known modern witch is Sybil Leek, who came from England to the United States recently and has had ample publicity during her sojourn here. She says that she wants to live quietly and not cause any sensations, but she appears in public in black capes and purple tights, so you'll have to draw your own conclusions about that. *Spirits, Stars, and Spells** says something so cute about her that I must quote it. Speaking of the articles in various American newspapers which tell about the doings of neighborhood witches, it says: "One of the most interesting of these articles was a story that appeared in 1964 about the British

* *Ibid.*

witch, Sybil Leek, who flew in from England—on a jet-propelled airplane, not a broomstick—to conjure up publicity for her book. The remarkable thing about her was neither her trappings—her capes and jackdaw 'familiar'—nor her pretensions to occult powers. It was the fact that the staid *New York Times* gave her twenty-two inches of copy."

I'm not as skeptical about Sybil's "occult powers" as the De Camps are, because, as I've said before, I've seen some rather curious incidents that keep me alert. Be that as it may, when somebody gets twenty-two inches out of the *New York Times*, I have to take my hat off to her.

Witches go back to the beginning of time, and witchcraft has been practiced all over the world in all ages and in all cultures. Archeologists have found a grave in Denmark dating from the Bronze Age which contained artifacts indicating that the little woman who was buried there was very important, for costly swords and gold jewelry were buried with her. But she was also a witch. Beside her were the identical tools used in witchcraft today: a bronze bowl containing an iron knifeblade, the claw of a lynx, bones of a weasel, vertebrae of snakes, twig of rowan, and a bronze thread—all part of the magic of her modern counterparts.

In some of the earliest written documents witchcraft is mentioned, and it has its roots in many early religions. The witches practicing in England today evolved their rites from the religious ceremonies of the Druids. Some witches claim to be directly descended from these early Celtic "wise ones." In fact, witches call themselves the "Wica," which means "the wise people." It has generally been thought that their powers were hereditary, and that the craft was apt to run in families. In former days many children were brought up to be witches. At one time sabbats, or meetings, were held quite openly, although in secluded clearings of the forests, and the merrymaking of the nude cavorters was a sight to see if you were adventurous enough to sneak out to spy on them. Witches may dance nude because it's more fun that way, but they say they do it because it builds up more "power." Power is the psychic force which makes their clairvoyance and their magic spells possible. 1507190

The horrors of the Medieval witch-hunts are widely known and I won't dwell on them here. Suffice it to say that from the thirteenth to fifteenth centuries and even later, the Inquisition conducted a campaign against what were termed the "forces of darkness." And what could be darker than a horrible old witch who cast evil spells and cavorted in the nude? Unfortunately, no one was safe from aspersions of witchcraft, even if he didn't know an evil spell from an awful incantation. Anyone who hated you could denounce you as a witch, and your goose was cooked. An estimated nine million people died during this time for alleged witchcraft. Even as recently as 1888 a woman was burned as a witch in Peru, and an Irishman named Michael Cleary burned his wife to death for the same reason in 1895.

Naturally, the real witches went underground when the Inquisition started, or perhaps many more would have been killed. They haven't surfaced since then, until this present uprising of witches in England.

In primitive societies, witch cultures have been holding sway in full force without cessation from the beginning of time. Illiterate tribesmen seek some agent on which to blame their illnesses, misfortune, and even death. The witch is a natural scapegoat. Witch doctors, or those who protect the natives from these dangers, are among the most influential men in every tribe.

Once in a while it turns out that a witch doctor is really a witch himself. An interesting story about such a person comes from Major C. Court-Treatt.* In 1921 Major Court-Treatt had established a rest camp in Bandala country, along the border between Sudan and French Equatorial Africa, and there had managed to acquire the enmity of the local Karogi, or witch doctor. Since he'd had some slight training in medicine and surgery and was helping the natives without charge, the Major was robbing the witch doctor of fees and also whittling down his prestige.

The first evidence the Major had that he was hated came when he found the Karogi's small boy helper collecting his newly-trimmed hair and fingernail clippings. The Major writes: "I did not take the witch doctor's enmity lightly; magic or trickery, call it what you will, can be dangerous and it seemed that his tricks and spells began to work. At first it was odd things, small things, but yet annoying. Little objects disappeared. Water jars were found leaking. Tent pegs were pulled from the ground with only the strain of a slight wind, and tents fell."

Then Court-Treatt's pet animals, which he had collected in the wilds and was trying to raise, began to die one by one. Finally he himself began to feel weak and ill. He says, "It is hard to describe the sickness which

* *True Stories of the Strange and the Unknown*, Paperback Library, New York, 1965.

came upon me so gradually. It started with just a feeling of laziness. This got worse; every day I felt a little weaker. At first I hoped it might be sandfly fever but soon knew it was not.

"I had to admit that I was faced with the allegedly impossible. I knew the Karogi had used my hair and nail parings, probably in a clay model, in order to work some vile black magic upon me. I stirred my sluggish brain and fading energy to the point where I made up my mind to fight fire with fire."

First the Major found a way to entice the Karogi away from his hut, having some native make an appointment with him several miles away. Then he and a group of trusted retainers visited the empty hut of the Karogi. There they found a miniature tent just like his own, and inside it, he says, "I was horrified, but not surprised, to see a devilishly clever wax figure of myself spread-eagled and pinned upon the ground with long needle-sharp thorns from the Thal tree. These thorns are not only sharp, but somewhat poisonous; their prick causes an aching pain for hours."

The Major quickly set about a counter operation, and slung an effigy, which he'd had made of the Karogi, by a rope from the roof poles. The hands were tied out sideways to wall poles of the hut and the feet were pegged to the ground with two sharpened stakes. "From my haversack I produced four of the long razor-sharp hunting knives used by the Arabs," Court-Treatt says. "One, I drove to the hilt into the image between the eyes, one into the throat, one where the heart would be, and one into the stomach. All this was done in a great hurry for the Karogi might return at any moment."

As they left the foul smelling hut they tied the door exactly as it had been, but arranged so that when the door was opened it would fall forward into the face of anyone trying to enter. After they left the hut, the chief priest, Fiki, continued a monotonous praying for a long time.

"Suddenly the night silence was rent by a succession of screams. Screams of horror, fear, rage, and terrible curses were followed by the sound of a body plunging wildly through the brush." The Karogi's hut was then suddenly burned to the ground as the Karogi thrashed through the brush. "Suddenly we heard the most terrible prolonged scream of rage and fear that it ever has been my luck or misfortune to hear," the Major says. They went toward it and discovered the body of the Karogi. He lay spread-eagled on his back and a great Arab hunting knife had been driven through his heart, pinning him to the ground.

Court-Treatt concludes, "Silent and strained by our terrible night we started the short trek back to camp. As we walked I realized that a change was coming over my whole body. It was like a drink of old French brandy. The world seemed alive again and I was returning to it."

As we now come crawling out of the fetid African jungle, let us face the fact that modern America is not entirely free of witchcraft. Not long ago the Buffalo, N.Y. *Courier-Express* carried an article about a druggist who had been besieged for counter charms by those who believed spells had been cast on them by witches.

Hex signs are colorful geometric devices used to decorate the barns of Eastern Pennsylvania, the area inhabited largely by the Pennsylvania Dutch. These hexerai may have certain religious symbology, but their use is widely believed to have one important function: keeping the barns and their contents from being hexed by witches.

Pennsylvania Dutch lore is brimming with accounts of the effects of witches. As one example of this awareness, we have the 1928 account of John Blymire of York, Pa., who hacked and burned Nelson Rehmeyer to death. It was Blymire's belief that Rehmeyer was an antagonist, guilty of hexing him and refusing to give up his book of magic spells.

Many persons have seen an individual, possibly of Italian or Sicilian background, extending his first and little fingers and directing the sign of the "evil eye" at someone he wishes to tease. Teasing or not, the evil eye is taken seriously by many. As recently as November, 1965 a reader of *Fate Magazine* wrote a letter to the editor, asking for someone who knew how to help people who are sick from the "evil eye." He said that his mother had lost over sixty pounds, could eat very little food, and had become ill and weak, but the doctors could find nothing wrong and the hospital tests could not locate any cause. Who is to say that this woman might not have been suffering from a curse put on her by a neighbor or acquaintance who disliked her? We can only hope someone was able to suggest something to help her, for if she still believes in the ancient art of witchcraft she will just as surely believe in a spell to refute it.

CHAPTER SIX

Unidentified Flying Objects

From well-identified flying objects—witches on broomsticks—we turn now to strange sightings in the sky for which no really acceptable explanation has yet been found. Some of us will agree with the Reverend William Booth Gill of Bonai Mission, New Guinea, who said, "Before my own sightings, I thought a UFO was a figment of imagination or some electrical phenomenon." He changed his mind, as many others have done, when he personally became involved, and not until then.

It was in June, 1959 that Mr. Gill, an ordained priest of the Church of England and a graduate of Brisbane University, Australia, saw a flying saucer in New Guinea. He was sure he wasn't deluded because thirty-seven other people were present at the time and they all saw the same thing Gill saw. At first it appeared like the planet Venus, but it sparkled too much, and then it became very bright. Soon it came quite close and he could see that it was a disc-like craft with superstructures on top of it; like the bridge of a boat. Underneath it had four legs in pairs, pointing downward diagonally and looking rather like tripods.

Mr. Gill told reporters later that the object came down to about 400 feet, maybe more, maybe less. "It is very difficult to judge at that time of night and, not having experience in measuring elevation, it is purely guesswork," he said, "but as we watched it men came out from this object, and appeared on the top of it on what seemed to be a deck on top of the huge disc. There were four men in all. All those . . . who are quite sure that our records were right . . . signed their names as witnesses of what we assume was human activity or beings of some sort on the object itself." During the time the saucer was near them, the Reverend Mr. Gill and the natives signaled to the men on it and received similar signals in return. They hoped it would land, but although it came quite close, it did not.

In case one might suspect that we were being spoofed, even by such a responsible personage as a priest of the Church of England, let us remember that a variety of others of no less authority have also seen UFO's, including some commercial and United States Air Force and Army pilots. They've reported experiences near enough to that of Mr. Gill to make us wonder.

It is true that some people may be deluded into thinking they have seen flying saucers; some others may be trying to rib us with their stories. But the large number of sightings, the frequent similarity of them, and the undoubted integrity of many who have witnessed them, add value to all the reports.

I personally have not seen a flying saucer. But since I've been interested in psychical phenomena I have seen many other curious things. An object which suddenly appears in a closed room where it had not been a moment before (as apports do) is just as supernormal as a UFO. When one has seen apports, one's mind becomes more receptive to flying saucers, even though one attempts to retain his critical faculties and objectivity when dealing with them. We wonder why some people seem to be so gullible that they will believe anything. Perhaps it is because they once were forced by circumstances to believe something so incredible that nothing can be beyond the bounds of probability for them. I am sure this must be what happened to Sir Arthur Conan-Doyle, who studied psychical phenomena skeptically for twenty years. However, once he was finally convinced, by suprisingly sound evidence, he left his critical faculties at home for the rest of his life and accepted everything he saw verbatim.

Jacques Vallee says in his new book *Anatomy of a Phenomenon*, "I have always kept an open mind and have been careful not to reject extreme hypotheses merely on the ground of their 'fantastic' character, for nothing can be more fantastic than a natural phenomenon not yet recognized and classified by the human mind."*

Vallee says the legend of the flying discs has appeared throughout history. Apparitions of strange objects in the sky have for centuries stirred popular emotion and have at times caused crises and panics. Granite carvings on a Hunan mountain in China, possibly made as early as 45,000 B.C., depict people with large trunks, and cylindrical objects in the sky on which similar beings are seen standing. Sculpted rocks in the Sahara desert which contain similar carvings have been dated at 6000 B.C. The fiery sphere

* Henry Regnery Co., 1965.

seen by the prophet Ezekiel may well have been a type of flying saucer.

The name "flying saucer" was apparently first applied on January 24, 1878 by John Martin, a Texas farmer who saw a dark flying object in the shape of a disc cruising high in the sky at a wonderful speed. Seventy years later another man, Kenneth Arnold, also spoke of flying saucers, and this time the word was here to stay.

It seems that the phenomenon is also here to stay. We hear of new sightings constantly. Although I've spoken of the similarity, some of the countless descriptions of unidentified flying objects vary considerably from others. Instead of being disc-shaped, many are said to be cigar-shaped, or rotating flaming balls. When living entities have been seen, they may have been anywhere from normal earth-types to little green Martians, or bubble-eyed, flap-eared folk from outer-space fiction.

However, the likeness of some accounts is quite singular. Listen to the description of a UFO seen near Weeki Wachee Springs, Florida in broad daylight on March 2, 1965, by John Reeves, a sixty-six-year-old retired long-shoreman. It was a reddish-purple and bluish-green saucer-shaped object when he noticed it sitting on the ground. A 5-foot tall being in a silver suit walked toward it. When he saw Reeves he stopped, stood examining him deliberately for about two minutes, then reached into his left side and produced a black object 6 or 7 inches in diameter. Raised to chin level, the object flashed a brilliant light. Reeves believes it may have been some kind of camera. After taking another picture of him, the entity returned to the saucer, and a roaring sound became audible. "This shortly was replaced by a whistling sound. The rim began to revolve. The saucer elevated. The four stilt-like legs upon which the UFO had been resting were drawn up against the belly of the craft and slid out of sight into the ship. Within ten seconds it had accelerated straight up out of sight," Mr. Reeves said.* Sounds very much like Mr. Gill's sighting, doesn't it? And there's a long way between New Guinea and Florida.

Both these areas are a considerable distance from Antarctica. But the saucers have been seen there recently, too. On June 18, and July 3, 1965, members of the garrison at Chile's Pedro Aguirre Cerda Base reported an unidentified flying object, and at the same time the Argentine Navy garrisons located on Deception Island and the South Orkney Islands, both near the Antarctic continent also saw it. The Chilian Base Commander, Mario Janh Barrera, was contacted by radio and gave an interview to the press. He said: "It is nonsense to say that we saw a flying saucer like those from science fiction stories. What we sighted was something real, a solid object which was moving at incredible speeds, performed maneuvers, emitted a greenish light, and caused interference in the electro-magnetic instruments of the Argentine base situated close to ours, on a small island.

"Its red-yellow color changed to green and orange. It was flying at a short distance from the base at an elevation of 45 degrees, over the north of the island, and moving in a zigzagging course.

"It hovered in mid-air after performing one of its

* "Did a UFO Land in Florida?" by Coral E. Lorenzen, *Fate Magazine*, October, 1965, Vol. 18, No. 10.

maneuvers, remaining motionless for about twenty minutes and then moving away at high speed. We observed this object through high-power binoculars.

"I don't believe it could be an airship of terrestrial manufacture. As an officer of the Chilean Air Force, my knowledge about man-made machines gives me absolute conviction that nothing similar exists on the earth: in shape, velocity, and mobility in space."*

The Chilean officers say they took pictures of the object, but they lack proper equipment to develop them; so not until spring, 1966, when ships will put in at the base, can the negatives be sent out for developing. When they are developed will we hear any more about them? Or will the world be protected from an unexplained phenomenon, as the typical saucer fanatics will argue, because authorities think we might become upset about such things?

As Jacques Vallee concludes: "Through UFO activity, although no physical evidence has yet been found, some of us believe the contours of an amazingly complex intelligent life beyond the earth can already be discerned. The waking spirit of man, and the horrified reaction of his too-scrupulous theories, what do they matter? Our minds now wander on planets our fathers ignored. Our senses, our dreams have reached across the night at last, and touched other universes. The sky will never be the same again."

I'll go along with that.

* Scientists Photograph UFO's in Antarctica," by Coral E. Lorenzen, *Fate Magazine*, December, 1965, Vol. 18, No. 12.

CHAPTER SEVEN

Reincarnation

"If a man die, shall he live again?" We all wish to believe that he will. But where? How? Will a continued existence in spirit planes be enough? Not, for most of us, if one has merely to sit on clouds and strum harps. People who think about a life after death want it to be a new opportunity—the chance to make recompense for the wrongs they have inflicted in this life and to realize the benefit of opportunities they have missed.

And so the concept of reincarnation of the soul into other bodies which live on earth has great appeal for many persons. The accepted philosophy of some six hundred and fifty millions in the Orient, reincarnation is fast being adopted by most occultists and many spiritualists in the Occident as well. Why does the idea that we live many times on earth fascinate so many people? Let us see if we can analyze it a bit, and come to understand it.

The Bridey Murphy case is responsible for the rise of much popular interest in reincarnation in America. Maurey Bernstein, a Colorado businessman, discovered what many other individuals have discovered but have not had the wit to write a best-selling book about: when a hypnotized person is regressed, or told to go back mentally to a period of time before his life on earth, he may tell fantastic stories about other people. And if the idea is suggested to him, he frequently will claim to have actually been these people in previous incarnations or lives.

The concept put forth in *The Search for Bridey Murphy* by Maurey Bernstein appealed to many who were looking for answers to the injustices of the world. If one could believe his unhappiness was due to a karma or sum of actions he had chosen in order to make amends for errors in his previous lives, then he could understand better the reason for his inability to overcome his problems now. To some, it seems like justice to be able to blame your own former acts for your present difficulties. To others, of course—and your writer is among them—a God who would inflict constant repetition of earth lives on people who were not consciously aware of what they were doing to make recompense for past wrongs would be the most callous and inhuman of Gods.

If reincarnation were the only theory of an afterlife which allows one to make restitution and enjoy compensations, I might be inclined to feel that I had to go along with it; but fortunately there is the picture drawn for us by Emmanuel Swedenborg, a Swedish philosopher and theologian, who believed he had daily visits in spirit realms and came back with much information about conditions there. And there is the Evolutionary Progression theory as discussed by Stewart Edward White and others, an explanation, in a way, and a clarification of Sweden-

48

borg's ideas. All this makes much more sense to me than reincarnation.

However, it is only fair to allow the reincarnationists to have their say. We will, of course, accept the premise the man does have a soul which survives him after bodily death. Unless that concept is stipulated, there is no use going into any discussion of what survives and why and how. But anyone who is familiar with the evidence of psychical research, or who believes on the grounds of religious faith that man is a soul or spirit inhabiting a physical body while on earth, will wonder what becomes of the soul after death. Reincarnation says that it lives again on earth. Theories of reincarnation vary, some saying only a few lives are necessary in which to learn one's lessons; others claiming that the soul spins round and round again in a chain of births and rebirths—a veritable Wheel of Life, as it is called.

Vast numbers of those living in poverty in India, for instance, are caught and enmeshed in their philosophy, which causes them to feel hopelessly that they almost never will escape from constantly repeating their unhappy lives on earth. This is because they believe the cycle never is completed until a state of Nirvana is reached. Nirvana is considered to be a state of perfect beautitude which takes more quiet concentration than most people are ever able to achieve.

On the other hand, it must be admitted that some of the most noble of mankind's philosophical thinkers embrace reincarnation. "The theory of rebirth," as DeWitt Miller says in *Reincarnation the Whole Startling Story,**

* Bantam Books, N.Y., 1956.

49

"gives solace and understanding today to innumerable minds which otherwise would have been driven beyond the point of no return by the chaos, injustice, and stupidity of life on this strange and baffling planet. Religious leaders and profound philosophers have found in the doctrine of reincarnation a solution to the puzzle of what is God's will."

It may be surprising to some to know that in Brazil a substantial part of the entire population of nearly 65,000,-000 people believe in reincarnation. The philosophy was introduced in Brazil by a Frenchman born in 1804 who called himself Allen Kardec. His real name was Léon Denizarth Hippolyte Ravail, and he was the son of a prominent French barrister. A very serious-minded child prodigy, he was throughout his life hardly ever known to laugh. When spiritualism first spread to Europe, he became interested in table tipping—it was quite a fad for a while. He had no psychic gifts of his own, but he enjoyed sitting in when others played at the game of communicating.

But whenever Ravail was present, the messages became turgid and dull, turning into occult treatises which were supposed to come from very high spirit entities. These allegedly enlightened persons said they were giving him special revelations in order to enable him to fulfill an important high religious mission, and naturally Ravail's vanity ate up that information. When he was told that he must use the pseudonym Allan Kardec in his writings, he didn't hesitate to do so. As time went on, he received a vast amount of material through ostensible spirit communication which maintained, not inappropriately, that man does survive death and is able to communicate with those on earth. But it was also always added that the dead return again and again to earthly bodies through reincarnation. This last was the thing that distinguished Kardec's dispatches from those received by most spiritualists, and that is why he decided to call his sect "spiritism" to set it apart.

Kardec eventually published all the data he had received, and his books took France by storm. His persuasive and charming writings soon made him the chief advocate of spiritualism (although he hated that word) in all of Europe, and he acquired such a reputation in Brazil that he has become almost a national hero there. In 1957 the Brazilian government issued a stamp bearing his portrait, a round-faced, goateed, balding little person whose picture carried the legend: "Brazil . . . 1957 . . . First Centenary of Organized Spiritism."

As he had become more prominent, Kardec had also turned into something of a dictator, excluding from his circle of friends all mediums whose communications did not support his ideas on reincarnation. (One of the most curious things about all this is that about half of the mediums in the world transmit information that reincarnation is a fact, and material received through the other half maintains that it is a fallacy.) Kardec's interpretation had certain basic concepts which made many people unhappy to contemplate—even many who believed in reincarnation. Some of his controversial points are as follows:

The road of life is a long one, reaching back into an infinite past and winding on into an infinite future. When a person dies, he returns to the spirit world for a period of time during which his whole past series of incarnations unrolls before him in order that he may see all his mistakes. This makes him eager to try a fresh incarnation so he can rectify them. And back he goes, into another body, through all the trials and tribulations of earth life again.

To Kardec's critics this is a cheerless prospect of a terrifyingly and cruelly prolonged ordeal. Since reincarnation usually presupposes a complete loss of conscious memory of past lives each time he is on earth again man loses his sense of personal identity and becomes an entirely new individual in each incarnation.

Believers will tell you that the individual's subconscious mind carries on his initial identity, with ramifications and additions from each life throughout the entire period of time he spends on earth. To the faithful, this process is a palatable concept, even if an individual does not consciously have the opportunity to apply the lessons he has learned in past lives to his present incarnation. How the individual may bring together into one integrated whole consciousness all the separate consciousnesses he has embodied in all his incarnations, Kardec and others have never pointed out. They seem to presuppose some sort of magical melding of all the personalities of all the lifetimes into one highly evolved individual, come the ultimate point at which the spinning cycle ceases.

Another thing which drew fire from Kardec's opponents was his theory that a man immediately loses contact with his wife, family, and friends forever when he dies. Should he meet in a future life those he has loved in past incarnations, he would not know them. Maybe Allan Kardec didn't like his relatives, but some people do and want to keep in touch with them indefinitely. Most in this country who believe in reincarnation entertain the belief that they will constantly meet the same people, over and over again, in different lives. When rapport occurs with someone you have just met, it is because you were once lovers, husband and wife, or parent and child in another life or series of lives.

There is no more ego fulfilling statement that one reincarnationist can make to another than, "You are obviously an old soul." This means that you've made the cycle many times and developed a lot of wisdom and character. If one who says you are an old soul also insists that you must have been lovers in another life, this is additionally heartwarming, especially if the individual who says it is an attractive member of the opposite sex.

One of the common arguments against reincarnation is that everyone who believes in it is sure he or she was once Cleopatra or Napoleon Bonaparte. I do not find this as true now as it once seemed to be. Proponents of reincarnation now feel that they have learned so much more through suffering than through having been great that they are quite willing to have been a galley slave, a Christian thrown to the lions, or even a Hindu untouchable.

Dreams of past lives or memories during meditation in a trance-like state give confidence in reincarnation to many people. It is impossible to assure the dreamer that perhaps there was no actual significance, or the meditator that he was merely hallucinating. A vision of oneself in ancient Egypt is often accepted as more conclusive proof than anything else which can happen to one and, unfortunately, no argument is going to change a predisposed person who has experienced such an event. All the alleged logic in the world is not nearly so convincing as personal experience in any area of the psychic field, and it is especially true regarding reincarnation. How, then, does one attempt to explain these experiences away?

Well, there is the presumption, equally as supernormal as reincarnation, that perhaps a spirit entity is influencing you with his thoughts, and that you dreamed about *his* life on earth. Another explanation is that perhaps one is having a postcognitive extrasensory experience whence he sees by supernormal means an event which previously happened.

A well-known supernormal feeling called *deja vu* when one suddenly has a conviction that he has previously seen the same sight or lived through the same event he is now experiencing, is conclusive proof to many of reincarnation because of the belief that the sight or experience took place in a former life. *Deja vu* is just as likely to occur when stepping into a newly built house, however, as an old one. This makes the whole thing very confusing. If one attempts to attribute this to extrasensory perception, perhaps a precognitive dream about the place or event is the answer. Or perhaps one had an out-of-body experience and visited this spot. None of these answers are very convincing. The world is full of strange mysteries which are difficult to explain. Most of us overlook them and pretend they don't occur. That way we don't have to bother explaining them.

Further professed evidence for reincarnation, for which it is difficult to offer a satisfactory alternative explanation, is the existence of people who have memories of past lives. Children frequently relate stories of previous events on earth which are sometimes so compelling as to raise many more questions than they answer. I won't go fully into the story of Shanti Devi here; I've talked about her in several other books. Suffice it to say that she was a little girl who was born in Delhi in 1926. From the time she was four years old onward she told her parents she was the wife of a man in Muttra. When she was finally taken there, she identified her former husband, all his relatives, his home, and the parents of his wife who had died. This was observed carefully and confirmed by many people.

Other stories crop up from time to time of boys and girls whose similarity to Shanti Devi is noteworthy. Sushil Chandra Bose in *Jatismar Katha'—a Book on Reincarnation* tells us about Vidyabati Devi. She was the Hindu wife of Mangal Deo Sharma and "the best wife a man ever had" according to her husband. "She is my salvation," he said. "She thinks only of how I may be happy, healthy, and prosperous." But when Vidyabati was a child, her memories were all of a man supposedly her mate in a previous incarnation. When she was less than three, she used to make mud patties and tell her mother to give them to Punditji. When asked who Punditji was, she said it was her husband. Now, everybody knows that children invent imaginary playmates, so her mother paid no attention at first. But eventually Vidyabati reported the name of her husband—Dr. Vasudev Sharma. She described his home in another city and her life while married to him. Vidyabati's mother ultimately learned that there really was such a man in that city and the details of his former marriage were exactly as her child had depicted them.

Sushil Chandra Bose interviewed Dr. Sharma when he was an old man, but he remembered Vidyabati well. He had been taken to meet her anonymously when she was seven years old. As soon as she saw him she put a cloth over her head as if she were in the presence of her husband. Then she whispered his name. She was able to identify so many things and to tell him so much that had been intimate between himself and his fourth wife who had died that Dr. Vasudev Sharma was firmly convinced that this girl had been that fourth wife.

Now, psychical researchers, whatever their own beliefs about reincarnation, find the stories of children who claim to remember past lives interesting and worthy of study. So many such cases can't all be fraud or wishful thinking on the part of families trying to make something of their children's games of make believe. There may be more realistic theories than reincarnation to account for them, and the researchers are trying to formulate some. So far they haven't been very successful.

Perhaps the answer, they wonder, is personification. Once in a while, a hypnotized person, such as Bridey Murphy, will tell stories purporting to be memories from a former life. Some investigators believe that they are merely personifying this individual, acting out the role to please the hypnotist. If the subjects happen to relate true facts about the life they are describing, it may be because they have read a book about that person or an old newspaper clipping published at the time of his death. They may then bury the memory of this information, and later personify it in their imaginings. This, it is said, would also apply to the children who claim to remember past lives. It doesn't explain the ones too young to read, however, does it?

Another theory to account for these alleged past memories focuses on the Akashic records, said to be cosmic records of all human events and deeds. Perhaps all human thoughts and actions are recorded on a constantly moving cosmic account of the doings of men and women. Perhaps then the child somehow taps this record to get his information. Perhaps!

Maybe C. G. Jung's universal subconscious (or collective unconscious) is the answer. It is probably just another way of interpreting Akashic records in terminology more acceptable to psychologists.

Professor C. T. K. Chari, of Madras Christian College in India, leans toward extrasensory perception as the answer to our puzzle. This strange capacity of the mind, he believes, may here be in operation in some form more powerful than we have yet perceived. He suggests that the child who has this information about another life might have obtained it, at least theoretically, "from the minds of those few persons who knew it, or by clairvoyance, directly from objects such as tombstones, court records, etc." There are experiments being conducted among parapsychologists which point to a comprehensive paranormal cognition of the general extrasensory perception type spanning the past, present, and future history of persons and objects. It would suggest that perhaps these children are unconsciously indulging in a post-cognition of some deceased person's life.

Yet again, asks Chari, "Why is a spiritist interpretation ruled out?" Chief exponent of the spiritist idea, or possession, was Dr. Carl Wickland, a physician in a mental hospital who wrote the book called *Thirty Years among the Dead*. Dr. Wickland says: "That the belief in reincarnation on earth is a fallacious one and prevents progression to higher spiritual realms after transition has been frequently declared by advanced spirits, while numerous cases of obsession which have come under our care have been due to spirits who, in endeavoring to 'reincarnate' in children, have found themselves imprisoned in the magnetic aura, causing great suffering to both their victims and themselves."*

In his hospital Dr. Wickland cured numerous insane persons by what he claimed was inducing the entity who was possessing them to leave their bodies. He did this by the use of a machine which produced static electricity similar to the shock treatment now used. The electric shock annoying the possessing spirit, or spirits, they were temporarily forced out of the body. At the time the shock therapy was administered, Dr. Wickland's wife, who was an outstanding medium, would become entranced, and the dispossessed entity would be allowed to enter her body. Then the entity would be questioned. He would be told that he had passed through the experience called death and had then entered the body of another. After this explanation had been given him, he would be told how to go ahead with his own life in the spirit world so that he would leave those on earth alone. Finally, he would also be asked how he happened to get where he was.

From his discussion with such entities Dr. Wickland concluded that persons who die convinced of reincarnation can sometimes cause incalculable damage not only to themselves but to others. Believing they must return for another earth life and not knowing how to go about it, they may enter the body of a living person and then not

* Los Angeles, Natl. Psychological Institute, 1924.

know how to leave. An individual with a weak personality, or one who has been debilitated by illness, or addiction to drink or drugs, may without being aware of it allow such an unenlightened spirit to take possession of him. Wickland says that in his hospital numerous insane persons were cured when the possessing entities were induced to leave their bodies.

The case of a five-year-old boy who suddenly began to behave like an old man is related by Wickland. The child began to speak of himself as being old and ugly; he lay awake nights worrying over trifles, muttering strange and dire presentiments. At times he had an uncontrollable temper, which was quite the opposite of his previous sunny disposition. When this child was brought into the presence of the medium, Mrs. Wickland, it was soon elicited that he had been possessed by the spirit of an old man who, believing he must reincarnate, had entered the body of this little boy. He had then discovered that he was helplessly imprisoned and incapable either of leaving or of making his presence known.

Well, perhaps some of these alleged entities got into such a pickle because they believed in reincarnation. Certainly the belief can't cause too many people this kind of trouble, though; and there are so very many who get good from it because it gives them hope for the future. The followers of Edgar Cayce alone have found a tremendous amount of solace from their belief. Cayce, known as "the Virginia Beach (Va.) seer," was a fundamentalist Christian who did not believe in reincarnation. But, oddly enough, when he was in a hypnotic trance state, he preached the doctrine. Cayce's prime work was devoted to psychic healing in which he, or, perhaps, as was claimed, a spirit doctor speaking through him, gave diagnoses and prescribed treatment for sufferers seeking his aid. It was not necessary for the patient to be present. Usually the work was done in answer to letters from persons who were sometimes thousands of miles away from the entranced Cayce. And yet the information given about the illness was often very accurate, and the healing treatment recommended was usually effective. At the Association for Research and Enlightenment in Virginia Beach, a foundation built up around Cayce's work and run by his son Hugh Lynn, there are thousands of records on file of the exact words spoken by Cayce in trance.

In the latter part of his life the entranced Edgar Cayce began to give what were called "life readings" which described a person's previous incarnations and in many cases claimed to show that various physical ailments or psychological problems were due to actions and conditions which had occurred in earlier lives. It is said to have been a study of Cayce's work which led Maurey Bernstein to make his investigation of reincarnation by means of hypnotism, thus starting the surge of interest and controversy caused by the famous Bridey Murphy case.

As to the conclusions I have personally drawn from whatever study I have made of reincarnation: I don't like it, as I said before. I am a believer that one incarnation in an earth body is enough for any man, and what he doesn't learn in this sphere he has ample opportunity to learn in future planes of life. I much prefer the teachings of Emmanuel Swedenborg that every human being is a new creation.

According to Swedenborg, each individual man is an

immortal spiritual being with a mortal physical body. The physical body is an organism by which the spirit makes contact with nature and the world about him and gains certain necessary experiences from the plane of matter. Apart from the spirit, the body is incapable of thought or feeling, and when the immortal spirit—the real man—is freed from the body by death, the body, having served its use, rapidly disintegrates. The spirit, mind, or consciousness, in its spiritual body, escapes from the physical at death and continues its life in the spiritual world, its everlasting abode. There it continues to work and learn and perfect itself. It never returns to another physical body to live on earth again.

Earth lessons are not the only lessons which must be learned in order to improve the personality and character, according to Swendenborg and many spirit entities who communicate through mediums. Too much emphasis on the physical body and earthly experiences seems to reveal a compelling materialism which demands bodily satisfactions over and over again *ad infinitum*, when after death it really should be mental and spiritual development which is important.

In Eastern philosophies it is contended that the true end of human existence is mergence in the Divine, with resulting loss of distinctive personality, or in the achievement of Nirvana, the absolute and final extinction of individuality without loss of consciousness. According to Swedenborg, as members of the family of God we are distinct individuals, and always retain our individuality, each contributing the value of his personality to the common good. God has a supreme purpose in creation which is no less than the establishment of heavenly human society in the eternal realm. All the discipline of this earth life has its own good purpose in our character development, but it is not everything. Spiritual rebirth, not physical rebirth, is the great end of our being, for only through its accomplishment can we enter into the life of the highest spiritual reality.

CHAPTER EIGHT

Mental Mediumship

Other than Emmanuel Swedenborg's word for it, is there any evidence for the teachings cited in the previous chapter? Those who have studied spirit communication believe that a great deal of the information which has come through mental mediums confirms Swedenborg's philosophy. People who say that nothing of any value has been received through mediums have just not taken the time to delve into the vast amount of material available.

For me to admit that I have been convinced of a philosophy by having so delved and so read would limit my usefulness as an objective writer on the subject. And, anyway, I am always so critical of everything I read and experience personally that I argue with it constantly. However, I have been favorably impressed by a good deal that I have read, and more favorably by the Swendenborgian material than that which argues for the theory of reincarnation. Until one has taken the time to study carefully the evidence for survival of the human spirit which has been received through mediums, he should in all fairness withhold criticism.

What, exactly, is a medium? He might be considered to be a telephone or telegraph between worlds. The theory is that the medium's mind is the instrument, with a spirit communicator on one end sending a message and a "sitter" on the other end receiving. If there should happen to be survival of some conscious element of the personality after death, it would be logical that this "element" would wish to communicate with its loved ones still on earth in order to say, "Please stop grieving for me. I have not left you. We will see each other again when you die and join me."

It is said that many people are psychic enough to be able to receive communications themselves without the aid of a medium. I know countless intelligent, rational men and women who claim to see or hear spirits or in some other way get messages from them. Perhaps you also know people who have such experiences although they haven't mentioned them to you. Believe me, they don't talk about it until they are sure they will have a sympathetic hearing.

Those who are not psychic themselves have to depend on the services of a medium if they wish to attempt to get this kind of assurance, or some evidence of survival after bodily death. The parapsychologist studies mediums as the anthropologist studies primitive races, or the geologist studies rocks. He has found much evidence for telepathy, clairvoyance, and precognition; and he has come across much other interesting material which he cannot yet classify. He is reluctant to admit that it may be evidence for the survival of the human soul, because that would not be properly academic. But he will come right out and say that he has found some things which he does not know how to explain.

Because the only means of communication from minds in the spirit world to minds on earth is another mind—the medium's—you can understand the difficulties of transmission and reception. The mind of the medium has to be got out of the way or "blanked" so that it won't interfere with the message. The best way to do that is to have the medium in a deep trance. But many mediums are unable to go into a deep trance, and many others do not wish to do so. Therefore, they go into whatever milder type of trance is possible for them, and then their minds act as filters for the messages coming through. If the medium is in an actual state of awareness, his conscious mind may resist what he is receiving, or try to explain it, or in some other way confuse the message. If he is not awake, the message may still be colored by his subconscious stored memories or thoughts on the subject under discussion. A deceased psychical researcher, Richard Hodgson, has said that trying to communicate through a medium is the most difficult thing imaginable. He likened it to the experience of two people on earth who might be attempting to send information back and forth to each other from opposite sides of the continent, each using as his emissary a dead drunk messenger.

I am beginning my discussion of mediumship with the premise that the mediums we will mention are honest. It is unfortunately true that some mediums are fraudulent, and that others who have true psychic powers sometimes indulge in a bit of fraud to earn their fees when their own powers are not operating properly. In wondering why they will allow themselves to do this, Professor Charles

Richet decided it was from pure ignorance. In his book *Thirty Years of Psychical Research*, he was discussing Eusapia Palladino, an earthy Italian peasant woman, who was one of the world's greatest physical mediums. She seemed to take a mischievous delight in trying to fool her audiences when she could, but she exhibited incredible wonders when so well guarded that she could not cheat. Richet said, "In the first place, simple rustics like Eusapia do not understand that simulation of a phenomenon is a serious crime; they do not recognize the enormity of the fraud. They say, 'People want phenomena; well, we'll give them what they want.' A lengthy education is needed before they can be made to understand how odious and unpardonable is a lie that brings wilful error into our poor efforts at truth, where there are so many involuntary errors."*

William James, probably America's best-known and most highly regarded psychologist, who was also an ardent psychical researcher, made a statement about this which is highly quotable. Also discussing Eusapia's propensity for cheating, he said, "Her materializations and general monkey shines are mostly humbug. But allowing for all the cheating, and all the hideous vulgarity, there remains a residuum which we can't explain."

It is this unexplained residuum which holds intelligent men once they have become curious about psychical research. If the conclusion eventually reached from this study is that communication is truly possible, and thus that there is genuine evidence for the survival of the human spirit, who can say that this might not be the greatest blessing mankind could ever receive?

* Macmillan, New York, 1923.

It is possibly true that for every sensitive who goes in for trickery there is another who would not be caught dead at anything the least bit debatable. We know this to be a fact about Gladys Osborne Leonard, Eileen J. Garrett, Leonore Piper, and other prominent mediums about whom there has never been a word of scandal during their lives.

Broadly speaking, mediums fall into two categories, mental and physical, although sometimes physical phenomena will occur during mental mediumship, and vice versa. Mediums may use varying degrees of trance ranging from a mild state to complete unawareness of what is occurring. Sometimes mental mediums do not go into trance at all, but may pass on information they have gained clairaudiently on clairvoyantly (by hearing sounds or by seeing pictures which reveal information the medium could have no normal way of knowing). Automatic writing is a form of mental mediumship which occurs when the sensitive holds a pen or pencil lightly and allows an alleged spirit entity to write with it or when he uses a ouija board. (I'm going to stop all these "allegeds" from now on. As a sincere researcher I am attempting to accept every bit of information for what it is worth and nothing more. I am trying to be critical all the way. But in our discussion let's take the entities at face value while we're dealing with them.)

We must first realize the fact that when automatic writing is attempted, especially by people who are not developed mediums, much gibberish results, with a lot of high flying, usually trite, literature of a philosophical nature. Sometimes this is signed by a great name from the past; and the recipient of such writing is usually quite set up about it. Whether this actually comes from the subconscious mind of the writer, or from low spirit entities, depends upon your point of view. Well-identified communicators maintain it is earthbound spirits who do the writing. Psychologists insist it is your subconscious mind. You may have your choice. Just be sure you don't believe that what you are getting is true revelation.

I personally know very few authentic mediums who will use the ouija board. They believe that it is not worth the chance one takes, for it is so easy for intruding spirit entities of low character to use. Mediums say that those who have not developed their psychic powers to the extent that they have spirit guides and controls to protect them from intruding entities, should not attempt to use the ouija board at all. So if any of you readers are encouraged by my writings to wish to attempt communication on your own, please go to a medium and sit in a development class for a while before you try anything alone. I don't want to be held responsible for a rash of neurotic, mixed-up kids throughout the country.

A few people who have attempted to use the ouija board, without having had any development of their psychic powers, have had highly interesting results, however. The famous Patience Worth story is a case in point. One evening in St. Louis, Missouri, in 1913, Pearl Lenore Curran, a housewife, and Emily Grant Hutchings, an author, sat, as they had sat many evenings before, with a ouija board on their knees. They had never before received anything of particular note, but this night the pointer suddenly became endowed with unusual agility and wrote: "Many moons ago I lived. Again I come. Patience Worth is my name."

68

As it turned out, Mrs. Curran was a latent medium, and Patience Worth was able to write through her for many years afterwards. She eventually spoke the letters (never words) instead of using the ouija board. She wrote many beautiful poems and several novels, all far beyond the natural talents of Mrs. Curran. And all she wrote was in the idiom of seventeenth century English, much of which is now archaic, obsolete, and dialectical. Her faculty for composition was of a very high order, and she could compose poetry as fast as the pointer could move across the board. Eventually hundreds of thousands of words were accumulated, all attributed to Patience Worth, whoever she was.

And who was she? If she was a strange personality, split off from Mrs. Curran's own mind, which never evidenced itself except when she was in a mediumistic state, it is a very curious thing. If she was what she claimed to be, the spirit of a woman who had lived several centuries ago, that is even stranger, is it not?

A much more recent experience of this sort also occurred to a woman who had no previous evidence of psychic ability, Grace Rosher. This Englishwoman is an artist of such caliber that her miniature portraits have been shown in the Royal Academy in London. She is not given to sudden flights of fancy, is honest, independent, and has a good sense of humor. She had no knowledge of, or interest in, automatic writing or any kind of alleged communication with spirits. "In fact," she says in her book *Beyond the Horizon*, "I was quite definitely prejudiced against anything of that kind, and had no wish to investigate the subject."*

* London, James Clarke & Co., 1961.

And yet one day as Grace was sitting at her desk with pen in hand, pausing to decide what to write next, her pen took it upon itself to make a statement. It wrote, as if of its own volition, "With love from Gordon." Thus began one of the most curious correspondences of all time, for Gordon Burdick had been Miss Rosher's fiancé who had died four days before, on September 20, 1957.

The romance between Grace Rosher and Burdick had been a long-time, long-distance affair, lasting forty years. When Grace was in her twenties, she had left her English home to visit in Vancouver, Canada. There she met Gordon Burdick, director of a shipping salvage firm. They fell in love and became engaged, but because of family interests they had to be separated. Grace returned to England, and Burdick remained in Canada. They wrote carefully restrained love notes to each other across the distance, but one thing after another came up to delay their marriage all those years.

Finally it was actually arranged for Gordon to come to London so that they could tie the nuptial knot; but a week before he was to sail he died. It was while Grace was penning the sad news to a cousin that the automatic writing from Gordon began.

At first Grace Rosher suspected that her own subconscious mind was writing the lines; but as time went on the messages became more and more complex, and Miss Rosher became more and more confused as to their origin. As both parties gained more facility at their task, the script grew to look just like Gordon's. And yet more odd, the communicator soon learned to write when Grace's hand was not even gripping the pen. She made a fist and leaned the pen against the outside of her thumb. Some force from her body, with no guidance from her hand, made the pen move, and soon entire pages of manuscript were being written in what appeared to be Burdick's own handwriting. (I well know that certain individuals have attempted to disprove this story by showing that it is possible to hold a pen in that curious position and actually to write of your own volition. That they can also produce script in any way similar to that of another specific person's has not been indicated.)

Grace kept her automatic writing a secret for some time, because, quite frankly, she was still not sure her own mind was not playing tricks on her. But gradually she began talking of it to some of her friends. Eventually the word reached the London *Mirror*, which sent an incredulous reporter and an equally unbelieving cameraman to investigate, and a handwriting expert named F. T. Hilliger to give the writing a careful examination.

Even in front of these witnesses the pen moved as usual. Apparently the spirit of Gordon Burdick had no stage-fright. In his small backhand, completely different from Grace's bold forward slant, the pen wrote, as previously, with only the back of her thumb touching it. The photographer got pictures of the pen in action. The reporter took notes of everything that occurred. Both of them were amazed, and they didn't hesitate to say so.

The handwriting expert studied samples of Burdick's letters before his death and compared them with the automatic script. He found them so similar that he wrote, "On a purely scientific basis this is impossible.

"Forgery and copying must be ruled out because they require laborious care—and this message was written with speed. I picked twenty handwriting characteristics which

71

repeat themselves in the letters Gordon wrote during his lifetime. Sixteen of them are reproduced consistently in the writing that has just occurred on these pages. That fact is staggering but conclusive."

An English medium named Hester Dowden had great success with automatic writing by pen and the ouija board. Communicators through her gave their names and information of a highly individual character, providing much evidence which has confounded skeptics and kept researchers busy trying to figure it out. Maurice Barbanell says of Mrs. Dowden in his book *This is Spiritualism:**

"To watch one of her ouija-board seances was an unforgettable experience. Messages would arrive at a speed of three thousand words an hour—and bear in mind that each word had to be spelled out. When she used her pencil for automatic writing, the rate was reduced to a mere two thousand five hundred words an hour. The majority of people will find that a thousand words an hour is as much as they can manage. It was not unusual for Hester Dowden to receive messages in foreign languages, in French and German, which she knew, and in Spanish, of which she was ignorant.

"The most striking communications that came through her hand were those claiming to originate from Oscar Wilde. Wilde's spirit signature was an exact replica of his earthly one. The handwriting disclosed his peculiarities. Events from his childhood days were mentioned and inquiry proved them to be accurate. The literary style, which is the acid test, was highly characteristic.

"It all began at a seance one night with the words: 'Lily,

* London, Herbert Jenkins, 1959.

72

my little Lily. No, the lily was mine—crystal thread—a silver reed that made music in the morning.'

" 'Who are you?' they asked. Immediately the writing began again: 'Pity Oscar Wilde—one who, in the world, was a king of life . . .' "

This sort of thing went on for some time, in beautiful prose, quite like Wilde's and quite unlike Mrs. Dowden's. Asked, "Why did you come here?" the writing replied: "To let the world know that Oscar Wilde is not dead. His thoughts live on in the hearts of all those who, in a gross age, can hear the flute voice of beauty calling on the hills or mark where her white feet brush the dew from the cowslips in the morning. Now the mere memory of the beauty of the world is an exquisite pain.

"I was always one of those for whom the visible world existed. I worshipped at the shrine of things seen. There was not a blood stripe on a tulip or a curve on a shell, or a tone on the sea, but had for me its meaning and its mystery and its appeal to the imagination. Others might sip the pale lees of the cup of thought, but for me the red wine of life. Pity Oscar Wilde. To think of what is going on in the world is terrible for me. Soon the chestnuts will light their white candles and the foxgloves flaunt their dappled, drooping bells."

The writing went on, "Soon the full moon will swim up over the edge of the world and hang like a great golden cheese." Then the words, "Stop! stop!" were interjected, and the communicator went into a tantrum. "This image is insufferable," he wrote. "You write like a successful grocer who from selling pork has taken to writing poetry." He was complaining because he could not find

73

the proper words in the medium's mind for his poetic expression, an example of the coloring about which I spoke earlier. Still forceful in his afterlife, Wilde continued his efforts until he got the word he wanted. "Try again," he wrote. "Like a great golden *pumpkin* hanging in the night." And then he was satisfied.

Barbanell goes on with a delightful account of some of Wilde's characteristic sarcastic retorts: "A week later, the automatic writing was resumed again. Dr. E. J. Dingwall, then research officer of the Society for Psychical Research, was present. Wilde, the cynic and merciless satirist expressed himself thus: 'Being dead is the most boring experience in life. That is, if one excepts being married or dining with a schoolmaster. Do you doubt my identity? I am not surprised, since sometimes I doubt it myself. I might retaliate by doubting yours.

" 'I have always admired the Society for Psychical Research. They are the most magnificent doubters in the world. They are never happy until they have explained away their spectres. And one suspects a genuine ghost would make them exquisitely uncomfortable. I have sometimes thought of founding an academy of celestial doubters . . . which might be a sort of Society for Psychical Research among the living. No one under sixty would be admitted, and we should call ourselves the Society of Superannuated Shades. Our first object might well be to insist on investigating at once into the reality of the existence of, say, Mr. Dingwall . . .' "

As Wilde's statement ridiculing researchers went on and on, Barbanell wonders: "Is there any literary man who could sit down and produce spontaneously similar writing at the rate of sixty to seventy words a minute, which is the speed at which the Wilde communication came? In one instance, one thousand seven hundred words, a long and logical argument, were written in about an hour and a quarter." Over a period of time this communicator calling himself Oscar Wilde wrote frequently, and finally he dictated a complete play. Without disclosing its authorship, Mrs. Dowden showed it to some theatrical managers. They rejected it because it was too much like Oscar Wilde!

When a medium goes into trance and messages are spoken through him, his master of ceremonies is called a "control." Controls usually claim to be children, or young foreigners who make cute mistakes in grammar or speak with a ridiculously funny accent, or in other ways insert humor into the proceedings. The spirit entities who communicate say that a state of humorous relaxation on the part of the sitters is very important for proper "vibrations" at a seance in order to make reception easier.

Feda is the name of the control of Gladys Osborne Leonard, one of the world's greatest mental mediums. Feda said she was a teen-age spirit, and she had a delightful personality. Mrs. Leonard, the most carefully investigated and documented medium of all time, is a truly great woman. Now in her eighties and retired from active work, she lives in Kent, England. Her personal integrity was such that her honesty was never questioned; but nonetheless, she always insisted safeguards be used. For this reason most sitters came to her anonymously, and at times detectives were even hired, with her permission, to make sure she could not have acquired by normal means the information she transmitted.

Many persons who attended Mrs. Leonard's seances

became convinced that they had communicated with the dead, and this was enough to satisfy them. But others sought to receive material so genuine and accurate that it would stand up to scientific analysis as survival evidence. Therefore, they established a framework of painstaking supervision and kept records of everything said in every seance.

Feda and the communicators through Mrs. Leonard attempted to devise certain tests which would in some way prove that they were the specific individuals they claimed to be, still surviving with memories and personalities intact. So they worked out "book tests" which they used extensively. Certain books available to the sitter, but from a library the medium had never seen, were used to produce personal messages from the communicators. The clues given at the seances were always unintelligible until the specific book had been procured and opened to the designated page.

A simple example of a book test was reported by the Reverend Charles Drayton Thomas, a Methodist minister who devoted the last fifty years of his life to psychical research and who kept careful records of every word that was spoken in the seance room. In his book *Some New Evidence for Human Survival*, Drayton Thomas writes:

"We had discussed the possibility of audible sound being produced by my communicator to attract our attention at home. He tried, but rarely succeeded in making knocks which might not be attributed to ordinary creakings in floor or furniture. One night, however, I concluded that a special effort had been made and that the result was a definite success; for thrice I heard a loud double knock. I noted the incident and added it to a list of such items kept for reference. Three days later, at an interview with Mrs. Leonard, Feda *greeted me* with the assertion that *she* had succeeded in coming to our house and giving raps there. A few minutes later the following book test was given: 'It is in a book behind your study door, the second shelf from the ground, and fifth book from the left. Near the top of page seventeen you will see words which serve to indicate what Feda was attempting to do when knocking in your room. Now that you are aware that it was Feda's attempt you will see the unmistakable bearing of these words upon it.'

"On returning home I found this book to be a volume of Shakespeare which commences with *King Henry VI,* and the third line from the top of the indicated page reads, 'I will not answer thee with words, but blows.' "*

A much more complex test was received on September 29, 1917 by Mrs. S. E. Beadon; the communicator purporting to be her late husband Colonel Beadon. Feda said:

"In a squarish room are some books, not quite in the corner, but running by the wall to the corner from the window, a row of books. Counting from right to left the fifth book . . . On page seventy-one will be found a message from him to you. The message will not be as beautiful as he would like to make it, but you will understand he wants to make the test as good as he can. On the same shelf is a book in dirtyish brown cover and a reddish book and an old-fashioned book."

The following points about page seventy-one were made, as Colonel Beadon attempted to show that he knew what was on that page which might apply to himself and to his wife:

* London, W. Collins Sons, 1922.

1. It refers to a past condition.
2. But has also an application to the present.
3. It is an answer to a thought which was much more in your mind at one time than it is now—a question which was once much in your mind, but is not now, especially since you have known Feda.
4. On the opposite page is a reference to fire.
5. On the opposite side is a reference to light.
6. On the opposite side is a reference to olden times. These have nothing to do with the message but are just tests that you have the right page.
7. On the same page or opposite page or perhaps over the leaf a very important word beginning with S.

The room proved to be the dining room of Mrs. Beadon's mother's house, where she was staying temporarily. Mrs. Leonard had never been inside the house. The room was not exactly square, but one end was squared, the other end octagonal. There was an old volume of Dryden's poems and the others as described on the same shelf. The fifth book from right to left was a volume of poems by Oliver Wendell Holmes, which Mrs. Beadon had never read. Page seventy-one, second paragraph, went as follows:

> The weary pilgrim slumbers,
> His resting place unknown,
> His hands were crossed, his lids were closed,
> The dust was o'er him strown;
> The drifting soil, the mouldering leaf
> Along the sod were blown,
> His mound has melted into Earth
> His memory lives alone.

Now the story back of this communication is this: Colonel Beadon was killed in action in Mesopotamia. He was buried by chaplain and officers the same night near where he fell. The officer in charge wrote that all traces of the grave had been carefully obliterated to avoid desecration by the Arabs.

1. The poem, called *The Pilgrim's Vision*, refers to early settlers in America—"refers to a past condition."

2. It has an application in this verse to the communicator's own case. He received reverent burial, his resting place unknown.

3. At one time Mrs. Beadon investigated the possibility of identifying the burial site with the help of the officers present and, when the war was over, of having it marked with a cross. Since she met Feda, and became convinced that her husband was still living in the spirit world, she has thought very little about that idea, not being as concerned as she was at first that his grave was unmarked and unknown.

On the opposite page is a reference to fire, to light, and to olden times:

4. Still shall the fiery pillar's ray
   Along the pathway shine,

5. To light the chosen tribe that sought

6. This Western Palestine, (referring to the journey of the Israelites.)

7. On the next page, the overleaf, the poem is called *The Steamboat* and so the important word there begins with S.

Now you can see that many more hits occur here than would be possible by chance coincidence. If you don't believe it, tell yourself that in a certain location on the next bookshelf you come to you will find a book referring to a certain subject and that on a given page you will find a message applying to seven given conditions. You won't hit even a few of them, I can almost bet. This has been tried by researchers endeavoring to determine whether or not chance might have been in operation in the Leonard book tests. Their results were totally insignificant.

Charles Drayton Thomas received many communications through Mrs. Leonard which were designed to prove precognition, or knowledge of the future, and to show information which went beyond anything which could be known by the medium or the sitter. These were called "newspaper tests," in which the communicator gave data which he said would appear in specific locations in a newspaper to be published the next day. The message would also bring evidence of the identity of the communicator, or of specific knowledge which he had.

The newspaper tests were given at seances held at 3:00 P.M. They gave information which would appear in the next day's London *Times*, which at that time had not yet been made up. Therefore, that early in the afternoon no living person knew where any items would be located on the front page of the next day's paper. It was Drayton Thomas' invariable custom to mail a copy of the newspaper tests to the Society for Psychical Research as soon as he left the seance room. He thus documented the fact that the information had been received the day preceding the issue of the paper to which it referred.

Although many much more involved newspaper tests were received, a simple example is the following. Thomas

80

writes: "Having been directed to the first page and rather more than one-third down column three, I was asked to look to the left where, almost in a line with that spot, would appear my name and a little above it that of my wife. . . . And within an inch of those names I was to see my wife's age."

On examining the front page of the *Times* the next day, Thomas saw his first name, "Charles," and his wife's name, "Clara," within one inch of each other. Just one and five-eighths inches above their names was the number "51," Clara's age until one week before when she had had a birthday.

No account of mental mediumship would be complete without some examples from Mrs. Leonore Piper's communications. This great medium was discovered by William James, and from then on she underwent examination constantly with never a complaint about the rigid controls applied by the psychical researchers. She performed automatic writing while in a trance state, sitting in a chair with her head lying forward upon cushions, her nose and mouth arranged neatly to the side so that she could breathe. The right hand and arm would then reach out, a pencil would be placed in the hand, and automatic writing would ensue which gave names, dates, and personal information about the lives of those purporting to communicate.

Investigators of mediums frequently have great fun. They almost feel that they are in fairyland half the time, when they keep seeing and hearing things which make them doubt their senses. When evidence is produced under controlled circumstances, there is always a feeling of wonder about it, of "pinch me to make sure I'm awake."

I'm sure Dr. James H. Hyslop, a Columbia University professor who was president of the American Society for Psychical Research for years, must have felt as if he were playing childish games when he went to Mrs. Piper wearing a mask. But he was attempting to devise the most controlled conditions, and had to do it so that he could be sure that neither she nor a possible confederate might recognize him. Dr. Richard Hodgson made all the arrangements for an anonymous sitter, and then Hyslop drove to the Piper house in a closed carriage, wearing a black mask completely covering his head. Fortunately, he wasn't observed by the police or he might have been holding his seance in the pokey. Hodgson, at the window, waved to Hyslop after the medium was in trance, and then Hyslop entered, tiptoed across the room and took his place in a chair *behind* Mrs. Piper.

Throughout the entire sitting Dr. Hyslop never uttered a word, all the talking being done by Hodgson. When the communication ceased, before Mrs. Piper came out of the trance, Hyslop left the room, entered his cab, still masked, and was driven away. Even had the medium been in a normal state with her eyes open, she could hardly have been able to identify the silent masked man. Yet during this series of sittings Professor Hyslop's name was given, the names of many members of his family, and Xenia, Ohio, the small town they had come from.

So much family history came through which was personally unknown to Dr. Hyslop that it took him over six months of continuous correspondence with relatives to verify it. Mrs. Piper told him his father's name, "James," and referred to many particularly confidential conversations he and his father had held together. He was told that his father had trouble with his left eye, that he had a mark near his left ear, that he used to wear a thin coat or dressing gown mornings, and that at one time he wore a black skullcap at night; that he used to have one round and one square bottle on his desk and carried a brown-handled penknife with which he used to pare his nails; that he had a horse called Tom; that he used to write with quill pens which he trimmed himself; and so on. The communications also contained favorite pieces of advice which were typical of Hyslop's father, worded in ways characteristic of his mode of speech.

About such communications, Hereward Carrington in *The Invisible World* makes a few comments of interest. He writes:

"Where did this knowledge come from? Here was a woman asleep in North Boston, telling of events which had occurred seventy years ago in the midwest, where she had never been. She certainly never obtained this information by means of her normal senses. Much of it referred to memories of those long dead, who claimed to be present, communicating this material. If it did not emanate from that source, whence did it come?"

Of course, many will claim that it all came from telepathy from the sitter, Hyslop, or from the other persons still living who knew the information. Funny that telepathy in the laboratory has never revealed such striking capabilities.

Carrington goes on: "Here is a problem for science— the science of the future, the coming science. It is a crying shame that psychologists today, for the most part, merely ignore and ridicule such facts, instead of investigating them and trying to understand them. For, on any theory, we are confronted with a problem of gigantic magnitude."*

* The Beechhurst Press, New York, 1946.

CHAPTER NINE

Physical Mediumship

Does the impossible really happen? Most of the topics I have discussed in this book would seem to indicate that perhaps, on occasion, it does. Now I am going to talk about the farthest-out subject of all—physical mediumship. In the presence of a physical medium trumpets may whirl about, heavy tables may be raised up into the air, objects may appear out of nowhere (apports), or materialized deceased entities may walk from the medium's cabinet, talk, identify themselves, and be recognized by their friends in the audience, and then melt into the floor. All of these things are said to have taken place in various seances held by strong mediums and to have been witnessed by reputable investigators under controlled conditions.

By controlled conditions I mean that the researcher has been allowed to search the premises thoroughly and examine the body and the chair of the medium, tie him up, and to do other things which would inhibit his activities in case he planned to practice deception. There is no known explanation for such phenomena by normal means unless fraud is the answer. So if it really can be proved that the possibility of fraud has been entirely eliminated, then the phenomena of physical mediumship must indicate something truly exciting.

Of course, to a Spiritualist the phenomena are completely normal and not at all difficult to explain. He says they occur through the operation of natural laws with which most of us on the planet Earth are as yet unfamiliar. He says that these seemingly impossible feats of the seance room are performed by spirit intelligences, deliberately staged by them to meet the challenge of those who demand evidence of their continued existence.

There is no doubt that when controlled conditions do not prevail, fraud may be perpetrated at times. The only experience I personally have had with an alleged materialization medium was unfortunately of that type. In the summer of 1964 I attended such a seance at a Spiritualist camp. I won't tell the name of it because I am fairly sure that honest phenomena occur there sometimes, and perhaps the medium in question may even perform genuinely on occasion. But every act of this particular evening was as phony as false eyelashes, and it was not in the least difficult to see through.

There were exactly fifty people there, and each had paid $5.00 for the privilege of seeing his loved ones materialize. After the medium entered his cabinet—a large curtained-off enclosure at the front end of the room—all the lights were turned off except one tiny red bulb high on the back wall. The room seemed pitch black until our eyes adjusted, but after that we could easily make out the forms of the people across the circle from us; and it was easy to see the materializations when they appeared.

I must admit it was all very stimulating at first. My friend who had accompanied me and I clutched each other in delicious excitement as a white figure slid out from between the curtains of the cabinet, wavering and fluttering about. But when it passed near us, it didn't look ghostly at all. It was obviously a human being draped in cheesecloth with a mask over its face.

"It's mother, dear," the entity said to the woman who had been asked to come to the center of the room to receive her visitors. "Don't you recognize me?"

"Oh, yes," was the reply, and it seemed to be sincerely meant. As the evening wore on I realized that at least some portion of those in the room really did believe they were truly seeing their dead relatives.

The entities came in two assorted sizes: medium size and smaller-than-the-medium size. The smaller one must have been a woman confederate who had come up through a trap door inside the cabinet. White was worn when they played the role of woman spooks, and black for the men. The faces of each visitor, when one was close enough to observe them well, confirmed my original impression. They wore rubber or plastic masks, or possibly stockings over their features, which hid any definite outlines, yet showed a vague indication of eyes, nose, and mouth. The same two voices were always heard, with variations as to the age and sex of the entity impersonated, and the figures undulated their arms and bodies in such a way as to make their robes look truly ethereal. Their shoes, which occasionally showed under the robes, had a much more solid and well-cobbled appearance.

My friend was particularly impressed when her mother,

who had been a very tiny woman in life, appeared. This was because she was now a good foot and a half taller.

When I was called to the center of the floor and asked whom in the spirit world I would particularly like to have, I must say I put on a great act. "Oh, do you think I might possibly be able to see my dear sister Marie?" I quavered in the voice of deep emotion.

"We'll try to bring her," said the woman who was acting as gatekeeper, ushering the spirits in and out of the cabinet.

My first visitor, however, announced herself as a grandmother. "Susy, dear," she called to me, "it's so wonderful to be with you again." (I forgot to mention that I had had to give my right name in order to get in to the seance because we arrived at the last minute and were refused admittance. However, when I identified myself, the prospect of having an author in their midst who might write something about them someday made them find room to squeeze us in.) As soon as my grandmother addressed me the beans were spilled. None of my grandmothers or great grandmothers had lived to know me as a child, and, anyway, they wouldn't have thought of calling me "Susy." It's a nickname I acquired in college.

Then came sister Marie, a tall, masculine figure dressed in women's white. "Don't you recognize me, dear?" she asked flitting about in front of me. It would have been difficult to do so, even had she been draped in real ectoplasm instead of cheesecloth, because I never had a sister Marie. I never had a sister. My mother never even had a miscarriage which could have been interpreted as having produced a sister who had been raised in Spiritland. Marie

88

was presuming that I knew her, so I went along with the gag and talked to her, but I was not happy.

My last guest at this seance was a famous essayist, who came to a fellow writer because he admired her work. We were on such intimate terms, in fact, that he introduced himself merely as "Ralph Emerson," leaving out the more formal "Waldo." He said he assisted me by inspiring my writing. I thanked him and admitted that he'd probably been most helpful with my passementerie, and he nodded in complete agreement. "Yes, indeed," he said, assuring me that he would continue always to be at my service. He hadn't caught on at all that my test word "passementerie" had to do with old-fashioned bead trimming instead of writing—and a real Emerson certainly would have.

Although I didn't make a scene about it, I was inwardly fuming at the insult to my intelligence the medium thought he was perpetrating. What kind of a gullible fool did he think I was to be taken in by such inept impersonations? If they wanted to be tricky, they ought to be subtle enough to make it a real challenge, at least.

But a genuine materialization seance, I understand from thoroughly competent observers, is quite something else again, and highly convincing. In his book *Thirty Years of Psychical Research* Dr. Charles Richet speaks from personal experience: "The materialized object is nearly always a shape of something human—a phantom. Sometimes, as with Eusapia, only a hand; sometimes, as with Florence Cook and Marthe Béraud, they are entire figures. Although the appearance of a whole figure is more dramatic than that of a stump taking shape behind a curtain, both phenomena are essentially the same. A warm, supple,

89

resisting, articulated, and apparently living hand identical with a human hand in all points is not more extraordinary than a human personality that looks, walks, and speaks. The difficulty is the same: the abyss between normal and metapsychic science is as great whether there be a big, half-formed hand of John King behind the curtain or Bien Boa rising from the floor in front of it.

"I shall not waste time in stating the absurdities, almost the impossibilities, from a psycho-physiological point of view, of this phenomenon. A living being, or living matter, formed under our eyes, which has its proper warmth, apparently a circulation of blood, and a physiological respiration (as I proved by causing the form of Bien Boa to breathe into a flask containing baryta water), which has also a kind of psychic personality having a will distinct from the will of the medium, in a word, a new human being! This is surely the climax of marvels! *Nevertheless it is a fact.*"

Shades of the alchemists—maybe this is how to construct a Homunculus!

Richet goes on: "These materializations are usually gradual, beginning by a rudimentary shape, complete forms and human faces only appearing later on. At first these formations are often very imperfect. Sometimes they show no relief, looking more like flat images than bodies, so that in spite of oneself one is enclined to imagine some fraud, since what appears seems to be the materialization of a semblance, and not of a being. But in some cases the materialization is perfect. At the Villa Carmen I saw a fully organized form rise from the floor. At first it was only a white, opaque spot like a handkerchief lying on the ground before the curtain, then this handkerchief quickly assumed the form of a human head level with the floor, and a few moments later it rose up in a straight line and became a small man enveloped in a kind of white burnous, who took two or three halting steps in front of the curtain and then sank to the floor and disappeared as if through a trap door. But there was no trap door."

In trying to ascertain what these materialized forms are composed of, Dr. Richet coined the word "ectoplasm," because the material emerges from the body of the medium. A chemical analysis of ectoplasm was made by a coworker of Richet's, Baron A. von Schrenck Notzing, a German physician who specialized in psychiatry and psychical research. He spent thirty-five years conducting hundreds of seance experiments, being fortunate enough to find several mediums who would cooperate with him fully.

On a few occasions von Schrenck Notzing obtained permission from the medium to cut off a small piece of ectoplasm for chemical and microscopic analyses. He found that it was: "Colorless, slightly cloudy, fluid (thready), no smell; traces of cell detritus and sputum. Deposit, whitish. Reaction, slightly alkaline." Under the microscope it revealed: "Numerous skin discs; some sputum-like bodies; numerous granulates of the mucous membrane; numerous minute particles of flesh; traces of 'sulphozyansaurem' potash. The dried residue weighed 8.60 grams per litre; 3 grams of ash."

As described by Maurice Barbanell in *This is Spiritualism*, ectoplasm is ideoplastic by nature and "is capable of being molded to 'manufacture' the equivalent of the human body. Its relationship to materialization is similar to that of protoplasm in all material forms of life. Though non-

91

material in its primal state, ectoplasm is somehow compounded by 'spirit chemists' until it assumes the equivalent of the human body, with a pounding heart, pulsebeats and warm, solid hands. It becomes a form that breathes, walks, and talks, and is apparently complete even to fingernails."

Ectoplasm comes out of the medium's solar plexus, or his nose, ears, or other bodily orifices. Many infrared or flash pictures have been taken of mediums with ectoplasm pouring forth from them, and of actual materialized figures. Some pictures have shown ectoplasm holding up a trumpet or lifting a tambourine.

A study of the mediumship of Keith Milton Rhinehart of Seattle, Wash., which was undertaken in 1958 by a group of prominent scientists in Japan, revealed certain uses of ectoplasm which are highly interesting. These chemists, physicists, and other outstanding men and women of Japan spent a great deal of money constructing a special foolproof chair and other equipment in order to investigate Rhinehart, and they photographed all of the ensuing phenomena with infrared movie film and still pictures. They afterwards declared themselves to have been fully convinced that all the manifestations they saw were honest and could not have been produced by fraud. One of the pictures taken at this time reveals a long ribbon of ectoplasm about five or six inches across leaving the medium's solar plexus, extending down toward the floor, then apparently flowing upward over the edge of a nearby table. On the top of the table the end of the rope of ectoplasm is fashioned into a tiny three-fingered hand which is gripping a pencil and writing.

Photographs of the late Jack Webber, a Welsh coalminer turned medium, reveal ectoplasm pouring forth all over his head, face, and chest, holding up trumpets, climbing a wall, and doing other curious feats. One of the most interesting things about the series of pictures of Webber is that several of them show ectoplasm leaving his nose and forming into a large blob on his shoulder or the front of his chest. This ectoplasmic ball is then said to be shaped by the communicating entities into what they describe as a voice-box, containing larynx, vocal cords, etc. For direct voice, the entities are said to use that rather than the medium's own speaking apparatus. They must get inside of it, somehow, if what they say is true. One entity, who called himself "Sparky" and was identified as a deceased friend by a member of the audience at one seance I attended, said that in using a voice-box, "I have to talk through some pipes." He announced that this was the first time he had ever tried direct voice, and it was a very peculiar experience.

"How does it feel?" he was asked.

"It feels as if I were in a baggy suit—made out of lead," he replied.

Barbanell says, "Proof that the spirit voice cannot be the product of the medium's vocal organ lies in the fact that, while the spirit voice is speaking, the guide can often be heard speaking through the medium's throat simultaneously."

The reason I am particularly curious about the construction and use of the voice-box is that I have tried so hard to figure out how Keith Rhinehart manages to produce all the direct voices he does under the conditions he imposes on himself. The spirit explanation for this is this ectoplasmic voice-box.

Dr. Keith Milton Rhinehart is probably one of the

93

best-known physical mediums living today. He has in the past done materializations and given other stronger evidence of supernormal powers, but at present most of his phenomena are direct voice, apports, and things of that nature. Most of Keith's seances are held in the pitch dark, and it is extremely difficult to place proper controls on a medium who works in the dark; but for a time I was allowed to put him under test conditions. The manifestations were similar whether or not the controls were applied.

The first session of Keith's I attended was held in the complete dark in a sealed room. Although two dozen white carnations dropped into my arms, and red rosebuds were handed to me inside a trumpet, I did not give them too much significance, because I had no way of knowing where they came from. So at the next apport seance Rhinehart himself suggested that the lights be left on. This is not often done because it is said to be extremely hard on this medium to produce ectoplasm in the light. After this seance he was reported not to have felt well for several days, and many of his congregation were furious at me for "trying to kill their beloved medium."

However, as I said, the suggestion that this session be held in the light was made by Rhinehart himself, and I cannot but give him credit for it. Before the meeting I was given the opportunity to examine the entire room, particularly the stage area, to make sure that no objects were hidden there. There is no basement under that part of the building, and the floor is covered with wall-to-wall carpeting, which is fastened tight to the stripping along the wall. The walls are of plaster with no recesses or indentations where anything could be hidden. I almost took apart the chair in which the medium was to sit, and found no trick arms that would come loose, no false bottom of any kind, no hollow legs or arms.

The medium's cabinet is in the outside corner of the room, which is at the outside corner of the building, almost against the street. The cabinet is the dark, enclosed area in which the medium must sit, it is claimed, in order to build up his power, and so that the ectoplasm may have a controlled area in which to form. Keith's cabinet is composed of two purple velvet curtains which are pulled out on a rack from the wall to make a square in the corner of the room. The top is about two feet down from the ceiling.

After my examination of the room, I asked two skeptical men from the audience to come up and search the medium. They stripped him of all his clothing and examined him carefully. (Of course, there was no way to give him an internal examination, to make sure he had nothing hidden within his body, but the nature of the apports themselves seems almost to preclude that.)

Keith then resumed his shorts and shirt and I entered the cabinet and tied him securely to his chair, with a heavy cord which frayed if one were to attempt to loosen it. His wrists and bare feet were tied so tightly that afterwards there were red grooves in them.

Now, in order that his audience will not think that he is practicing ventriloquism when the voices are heard, before going into trance Keith always has his mouth filled with water and then taped shut. After the seance is over he spits out the water to indicate that he has held it in his mouth all the time. On this occasion I gave him milk instead of water, which he still retained when the session was over. I placed a wide strip of adhesive tape across his mouth and made marks on it extending out onto his skin so that if the tape were removed it would be evident. This is also part of his usual procedure.

I have learned from experimenting, however, that it is possible to loosen the center of the tape and talk without disturbing the correlation of the markings. I also know that one can do a little talking with water or milk in his mouth, and that it is possible for some persons to swallow a fluid which they later can regurgitate. I am not sure whether it would be possible under these conditions for a variety of voices to be produced, ranging from very deep sonorous tones to children's prattle, and a beautiful tenor voice singing (when the medium's natural voice is a mediocre baritone), or whether conversation could be sustained for hours on end.

The room itself on this afternoon was illuminated by several ceiling lights and visibility was perfect. I sat in the second row of the audience, the front row of seats being vacant, and watched everything that occurred.

What did occur, in the light, with the medium bound and gagged, was apports. An apport is an object which appears after having allegedly been dematerialized from somewhere else and then rematerialized in the seance room. These are said to come from sunken ships, an old ruin, a large factory with such vast quantities of small, inexpensive objects that a few would never be missed, or something of like nature. Spirits seem to be awfully careful to do nothing really dishonest in the securing of apports. This is why, they say, that the amounts of green folding money a medium would appreciate having apported to him never appear.

96

Susan, the cabinet guide—the little spirit entity who acts as master of ceremonies—called out the name of each person in the audience in turn. Then she would pass his apport under the cabinet curtain for him, talking as she did about where it had come from, or what it was, or why it was particularly appropriate for that individual. I observed each object land outside of the cabinet before it was picked up.

On that Sunday afternoon, in the light, with the medium gagged and tied up, some fifty apports were dropped out of the cabinet, varying in size from tiny plastic discs and inexpensive items of jewelry, and scarabs, to a Mayan or Aztec relic of stone about two inches high, a plain oval rock almost two inches long, a jagged arrowhead three inches long, and several smaller arrowheads. My particular present was a bronze Roman coin from about the Second Century A.D.

I can only say that I saw these things appear under the conditions I have described. You may suggest that Susy Smith is just not as careful an investigator as she thinks she is, and that the medium duped her. Yet one can't help but point out that countless such seances in the past, with researchers much more competent than I, have produced even more curious apports. Once someone asked for a sunflower at a seance held in the home of the famous naturalist Alfred Russel Wallace, and a plant six feet tall with a blossom and roots with fresh dirt on them was apported into the closed and sealed room. The only way to account for something like this is to discredit the investigator, or else to admit that there is truly more going on in the world than we now understand.

All arguments aside, I am perfectly willing to admit defeat if anyone can show me a magician's trick which can produce this kind of evidence in the light with no properties on the stage. Until then I'm afraid I am going to remain quite enchanted with apports as a means of indicating the supernormal powers of a physical medium.

CHAPTER TEN

Fire Feats

Fire had no power on the bodies of Shadrach, Meshach, and Abednego. These brave men refused to bow down to a golden image, as decreed by Babylon's King Nebuchadnezzar, and were therefore cast into a burning fiery furnace. It was so hot as to slay their captors; but their faith in their own god was so powerful that Shadrach, Meshach, and Abednego walked around in the flames uninjured. Nor was the hair of their heads even singed.

Is this just folklore of the ancient Hebrews? Or is it gospel truth? Perhaps it is somewhere in between, a little bit elaborated in the telling. The story is particularly interesting to conjecture about in the light of reports by many explorers, missionaries, and travellers that in primitive countries they have seen natives walking on fire during religious ceremonies. Could it be that great faith, properly applied, does protect one from fire?

Then again, maybe it is a self-induced trance-like condition that is the necessary requisite. Daniel Dunglas Home, the great physical medium of the last century, was seen to hold hot coals, and even to place his face in fire, while entranced. I personally have watched Doreen Walker, a nonprofessional American medium, handle glowing coals when she was in a trance-like state.

When large groups walk on fire, is it because preconditioning by prayer and meditation has so heightened their faith that they can perform miracles? Or has this preconditioning put them into a trance? Whatever the cause, it is fairly well authenticated that many persons in many ages have handled or walked through fire without suffering pain and without any lesions of their skin. Of course, there are also many explanations for these feats as perfectly normal occurrences made to look magical by trickery.

It is said that the annual fire walking ceremony of the Fiji Islanders, called Vila Vilairevo, can easily be explained by normal means. First a circular shallow pit is dug and filled with dry branches and firewood. A torch is applied and then stones are rolled into the blazing pit and allowed to heat for half a day. Green leaves are next scattered over the white hot stones, causing clouds of steam to rise dramatically as the fire walk begins, and the natives leap and prance about with bare feet over the rocks.

The Fijians themselves believe that once long ago their immunity was bestowed on them by a certain god. According to legend, a Fijian chief whose name was Tui Nkualita, received the remarkable privilege for himself and his descendants because he dragged the god out of a deep pool of water by the hair of his head. One explanation of the feat could be that these people believe so firmly that they will be protected from the fire that they

100

are protected because of their faith. Another, and more popular, explanation is that they don't burn themselves because the stones are of volcanic origin and so porous that they don't retain the heat, and that the heavy green leaves protect the feet of the dancers. If this is the answer, how does one then account for the fire-walking ceremonies where such porous rocks of volcanic origin do not exist: in Tahiti, the Marquesas Islands, Trinidad, India, and Japan?

The beliefs and practices of the Dosadhs, a low Indian caste in Behar and Chota Nagpur, included fire walking. On certain special dates the priest was supposed to become inspired by the tribal god Rahu, who became incarnate in him for a time, and to walk over a narrow trench filled with smouldering wood ashes. Of course, we can argue with the anthropologists that this priest was drunk, doped with narcotics, that he had heavy callouses on the soles of his feet which kept him from feeling pain, or even that his feet had been solidly coated with heat-resisting fluids or water. Perhaps any of these things was true. We can't be sure it wasn't.

Did these also explain the fact that in Madras often fifty or sixty people in succession, when in a sudden frenzy of religious ardor, walked, ran, or leaped barefoot through a hot pit? Did they intoxicate or drug or dope themselves, and then hurriedly rub heat-resisting fluids on the soles of their feet? That might have been fun, but what would have been the point of it? Is there any advantage to participating in a religious ceremony to show your great faith if you first take steps which will keep the faith from being necessary? In 1854 the Madras Government instituted an inquiry into the custom to see if it was harmful to the populace. They discovered that it was not attended by danger and that instances of injury were not sufficient to call for government interference.

If native fanatics are not harmed by such practices, those with little faith who attempt to participate sometimes are. An American writer named Percival Lowell once walked across a bed of hot charcoal in Japan and was so severely burned that he was laid up in bed for three weeks. The priests at the temple in the Kanda quarter of Tokyo, dressed in white cotton robes and chanting sacred rituals, had been calmly walking down the middle of the fire with no hurt, and so Lowell had determined to do likewise. A traveller named Ernest Foxwell had carefully examined the feet of some of these priests both before and after their passage through the fire, and they were quite normal; yet the heat was so great that sweat ran down Foxwell's face and body as he stood near the bed of glowing charcoal.

Although this account comes from James Frazer's *The Golden Bough** written in 1913, the same ceremonies continue in Japan today. Walter Edward Millins of Wichita, Kansas, attended similar festivities at a Buddhist priest school three different times from 1960 to 1963 while he was in the Air Force stationed nearby. He brought back to the United States pictures he took of the proceedings held high in the mountains near Tokyo. He says the whole thing was very colorful, with great crowds and many flowers, and much drum beating and parading.

The event was a part of the initiation ceremony, whereby young priests proved their power over fire. An

* Macmillan, London.

area roughly in the shape of a quadrangle had been piled high with boards and green boughs, and kerosene had been poured over them to make them burn brightly.

"After hot coals were formed," Millins says, "the workers scooped the fire into large heaps of embers. There was a hypnotic chanting of the liturgy as the initiates marched in a circle around the fire."

As the procession continued, first one, then another, left the group and began his trial. He lighted incense, bowed to the fire, and then to the assembled people. His legs and feet bare, he walked over to a mat on which salt had been placed and stamped his feet in the salt as a ritual of purification. "This couldn't have been to protect his feet from fire," Millins said. "We all known how hot salt becomes when heated." Then the initiate goose-stepped across the glowing coals, raising his knees high with each step. Even so, according to Ed Millins, his feet sank down into the embers as he walked, and the hairs on his legs were singed. But his feet were never burned. Millins himself walked to within five feet of the fire, and it was too hot for him.

These monks are protected by their faith, presumably. Or perhaps they put themselves into a self-hypnotic trance. In the case which came under my own personal observation, it was definitely the trance state which was said to account for the immunity to harm. The first time I saw Doreen Walker of Seattle handle fire, she had not been able to get herself into a trance. Something about the poor fit of the new dress she was going to wear for the occasion had made her so upset that she hadn't been able to sit quietly and meditate in order to become en-tranced. After she entered the chapel and performed a

103

dance around the brazier of glowing charcoal, she picked up a few hot embers; but she dropped them quickly. She asked that water be poured on the fire to cool it, and then handled some of the blackened briquettes, which had red centers when broken apart, but were not hot on the outside. After a few more half-hearted attempts on her part, the ceremony was over.

Doreen's disappointment that she had not been able to put on a better show for me was evident; and I was assured that she had performed publicly once before much more successfully. But my reaction to it all was negative. If this was fire handling, I was not impressed. I left town shortly after this, my interest in the subject at a very low ebb.

When I unexpectedly returned to Seattle, another performance by Doreen was hastily scheduled. This time the results were much better. And her lack of success on the first occasion made her second attempt much more convincing to me. If she had been going to put on a phony act, she could just as well have done it in the first place, could she not?

This second time, a brazier of flaming charcoal briquettes was waiting in the lighted chapel when she entered. She was not in a deep enough trance at first, and once again the picking up and dropping of coals began. We could see that she felt desperate, and members of the audience encouraged her audibly. "Come on, Doreen, you can do it," they'd say. Finally she walked into the foyer and sat at a table for a few moments with her head lying on her hands. Then she returned, apparently in a state of withdrawal in which she had no fear of the fire.

Now she picked up the glowing coals as casually as if they had been pebbles on a beach.

Doreen was once a professional dancer, and her graceful movements as she wove in and out toward the brazier in time to the music made her performance colorful, especially as now sparks flew into the air around her as she tossed the hot coals back and forth from hand to hand. As she carried her embers up and down the aisle of the church, she offered one to me to hold, but I drew back vigorously. Later I went up and put my hand as close as I could to the fire in the brazier, but at six inches the intensity of the heat was too much for me.

Doreen did not have anything coating her hands, nor had they been chilled before her performance. And they were not burned afterwards. I have gone into detail about the efforts she made to show off her ability, because if it had been a slick, professional job it would have been much more suspect. When one is close enough to understand the problems and failures, success is all the more convincing.

Daniel Dunglas Home, the famous physical medium, was well known to be impervious to fire when in the trance state. It was said that Home could communicate the power of fire handling to others, if they had enough faith. Some who tried to accept hot coals from him without believing they would not be harmed, bore blisters from the seances.

An eye-witness account of Home's phenomena is given in *Experiences in Spiritualism with D. D. Home** by Lord Adare, the Earl of Dunraven. We can accept

* The F. W. Faxon Co., Boston. n.d.

Adare's statements as verbatim reports of highly unusual events, as we may also accept the reports of Sir William Crookes and others. Or we can say that Adare was a carefree young man, implying irresponsibility, and that Crookes was a very poor observer when it came to psychic phenomena, although a noted scientist in other fields. And we can toss in the idea that the others were all mass hypnotized.

By any standard, Adare's account is fantastic. He declares that when controlled by a spirit entity, the entranced Home went to the fire, poked up the coals, and, putting his hand in, drew out a hot burning ember, about twice the size of an orange. This he carried about the room to show off.

"We all examined it," Adare writes. "He then put it back in the fire and showed us his hands; they were not in the least blackened or scorched, neither did they smell of fire, but on the contrary of a sweet scent which he threw off from his fingers at us across the table. Having apparently spoken to some spirit, he went back to the fire, and with his hand stirred the embers into a flame; then kneeling down, he placed his face right among the burning coals, moving it about as though bathing it in water. Then, getting up, he held his finger for some time in the flame of the candle. Presently, he took the same lump of coal he had previously handled and came over to us, blowing upon it to make it brighter. He then walked slowly round the table, and said, 'I want to see which of you will be the best subject. Ah! Adare will be the easiest, because he has been most with Dan.' Mr. Jencken held out his hand, saying, 'Put it in mine.' Home said, 'No, no, touch it and see.' He touched it with the tip of his finger and burnt himself. Home then held it within four or five inches of Mr. Saal's and Mr. Hurt's hands, and they could not endure the heat. He came to me and said, 'Now, if you are not afraid, hold out your hand.' I did so, and having made two rapid passes over my hand, he placed the coal in it. I must have held it for half a minute, long enough to have burned my hand fearfully; the coal felt scarcely warm. Home then took it away, laughed, and seemed much pleased."

A statement quoted from the Countess M. de Pomar said that another person present, Lady Comm, extended her hands, saying, "I will take it without fear, for I have faith." She held the coal for at least a minute without feeling any pain, and it was then placed on a sheet of paper which immediately began to blaze and had a great hole burned in it.

Others who declared that they were present when such feats were performed were a former president of the Royal Society, Sir W. Huggins, and a man named S. C. Hall. Hall said that he had had a white-hot coal put on his head and his white hair gathered over it, but he felt no heat and his hair was wholly uninjured.

Some of these stories about Home were collected by Sir William F. Barrett, an early psychical researcher, who attempted to defend them in his book *On the Threshold of the Unseen*.* He wrote:

"It is impossible to explain this by some fire-resisting substance, surreptitiously put over the skin by Home, for Sir William Crookes, than whom no higher authority on chemistry can be cited, tells us he knows of no chemical preparation that will accomplish this; moreover, he says

* E. P. Dutton Co., New York, 1918.

he examined Home's hands carefully, after he had carried a live coal about and he could see no burning nor any preparation over the skin, which, he remarks, was soft and delicate like a woman's."

In case one might think that those present at Home's demonstrations had been mass hypnotized, Barrett says:

"At Nancy and other medical schools, where hypnotic suggestion is used therapeutically, it is invariably found that even the best subjects exhibit marked differences in suggestibility, one subject sees the suggested object more clearly and not quite the same as another. But in these marvels, recorded with Home, the witnesses were not hypnotic subjects and all perceived the same thing, and only occasionally did they receive from Home any suggestion as to what was about to occur. The manifestations are recorded by those present as having been sudden, startling, and usually unannounced.

"If suggestion on Home's part be the explanation, it must have been purely *mental;* and difficult as it is to suppose all present are equally susceptible to *verbal* suggestion, the difficulty is vastly intensified when we assume unspoken mental suggestion, acting equally upon all the spectators. Nor must we forget that the witnesses in some cases were total strangers to Home, and fully aware of, and on their guard against, any possible hallucination."

Well, I don't know. As I've said before, once you have observed such things personally you are more inclined to believe them. Until then, maybe you have to take them on faith. And if you have enough faith maybe you too will be able to handle hot coals—if you should happen to see any point in trying to prove to yourself, or others, that you can do it.

CHAPTER ELEVEN

Psychic Surgeons

In the Philippines or Brazil it's hardly chic to go to a doctor any more. You go to a psychic surgeon. This is supposed to be a person who knows how to go into trance and let great doctors from the spirit world use his hands to perform operations. When spirit doctors operate there is a small incision, no pain, very little blood, and no danger of infection. This is so fabulous, of course, that though many creditable people say they have seen it and have even taken movies of it, it is difficult to accept.

You'd think if there were claims that a man in Brazil or the Philippines could operate frequently and successfully with an unsterilized knife and always cured his patient's complaints, that doctors and scientists would be rushing to Brazil and the Philippines to isolate the man and observe his procedures to learn how he does it. That's what you'd think. But doctors don't operate that way. Scientists don't operate that way. They sit at home and say, "Fraud." And the police come and get the man and put him into jail.

That is what happened to Jose Arigo, the Brazilian healer. During the past year he was given a sixteen-month jail sentence for the illegal practice of medicine. It is understood that, because of protests which were sent to the Brazilian government from all over the world, Arigo is now out on bail, but his work of healing thousands of indigent citizens may now be curtailed seriously, if not totally disrupted.

Reports about Arigo have come from many persons, including William Henry Belk of Miami, Florida, who has visited several healers on both sides of the world, and Dr. Andrija Puharich of New York City, a medical man and researcher. These men were accompanied to Congonhas del Campo, the small town in the interior of Minas Geraes, Brazil, where Arigo lives, by George Rizzini, an English-speaking Brazilian journalist who has made a film showing Arigo at work.

Puharich has his own personal testimony to add to the Arigo story, because he underwent an operation by this psychic surgeon. Puharich arrived in Brazil with a tumor on his arm which was nonmalignant and which lay near the nerve which controls the movements of the little finger. Because contact with that nerve could cause paralysis of the finger, Puharich's doctors at home had advised that no effort be made to remove the tumor.

When they were introduced, Arigo was allowed to examine the tumor on Puharich's arm. "Who can lend me a knife?" he asked quickly. Accepting a penknife which was offered, he opened it, and then, without sterilizing it, grasped Puharich's arm and began to make an incision. The flesh opened and blood started to flow. Arigo then pressed two of his fingers around the incision and the tumor dropped out onto the floor.

"It was hard, very big, and covered with blood," reported Rizzini in *The Psychic News*, London. Later in his hotel Andrija Puharich was interviewed by Rizzini, who tape recorded their conversation. Puharich said that at first it felt as if the medium had touched him with his fingernail, but that he had suffered no pain at all. (I'm sure he couldn't help but have cringed a little, however: a doctor watching someone plunge an unsterilized knife into his arm.) The size of the incision was said to be much smaller than the size of the tumor which was removed from it, the cut being about 1 centimeter and the tumor about 3 centimeters in diameter and 1½ centimeters long.

"How would a similar operation have been done by a surgeon?" Puharich was asked.

"He would have made the incision at least the same size but probably larger than the tumor. Then he would have used forceps to keep the wound open, and with every care, so as not to touch the nerve in that region, he would have extracted the tumor."

After two days the resulting scar on Puharich's arm was almost invisible, just a fine thin line remaining.

"How do you explain this surgery without anesthetics?" he was asked.

"The mystery isn't only in the absence of anesthetics but in the whole surgical process employed by Arigo," was the answer.

The psychic surgeon's family name is really Freitas. Arigo, the name he adopted for his healing mission, means "the simple fellow," which indeed Jose is. With a simple farm upbringing, he can barely read or write. He married very young and has fathered six children. Apart from his mediumship, he lives a normal life, takes an interest in local politics, and is very much a family man. His only special dislikes are tobacco and alcohol. He works as a government employee on a small salary and his wife adds to the family income by sewing for local tailors. Jose never accepts any pay for his psychic surgery, and there is no "love offering" or collection box in evidence anywhere in his home.

As a small child, objects moved in Jose's presence without being touched—an evidence that he was a natural medium. In his early married life he began to hear voices and to experience trance. His first psychic operation is said to have been performed without his knowledge. The story goes that at a hotel he had met a Brazilian senator who was suffering from cancer, a fact unknown to Arigo. The next morning the surprised senator recounted how Arigo had visited his hotel bedroom the previous night. Speaking with a strong German accent he had told him he would operate on him, and had done so. The senator apparently had paid small attention to this ignorant native's shenanigans, until he later went to the United States for the operation he was said to need for cancer. There he was told that there was nothing operable; the cancer had apparently already been removed.

The German accent which Arigo had acquired in trance is said to belong to a Dr. Adolfo Fritz, a German surgeon who died in World War I. When entranced, Arigo is taken over by this doctor. His face is then pale, and his movements are abrupt. His eyes have lost their brightness. He speaks in Portuguese with a German accent, or else in pure German to those who can understand him. And he operates with dispatch and authority. Arigo's day begins (or used to begin before his arrest) at 7:00 A.M., when a queue of perhaps two hundred patients may

112

be awaiting him. He goes to work at the Unemployment and Pensions Bureau from noon to 5:00 P.M., and then he resumes surgery in the evenings. It is said that he has attended as many as two million patients, and that they always live after surgery and never have any infections afterwards. It is no wonder that the local doctors want no part of him.

Rizzini asked Arigo why the operations are painless even though no anesthetics are used. The answer was that an invisible light descends. It is a spiritual light which is greenish in color; and it anesthetizes the patient and sterilizes the atmosphere.

For those who do not need surgery, Dr. Adolfo Fritz diagnoses, more often without even examining the patient, and writes long and intricate prescriptions with great speed, combining ancient and modern drugs in a way that is quite out of fashion medically. Then, with an imperious wave of his hand, he dismisses the patient.

It will be interesting if we can learn the latest developments in Arigo's case, and whether he is allowed to resume his practice. In the meantime, in the tiny village of San Fabian on the island of Luzon in the Philippines there is a man known as Brother Eleuterio Terte who has a large following for the same reason: he reaches into the bodies of living men and women and withdraws diseased organs and tissues, using only his psychic powers. In an article called "I Witnessed Terte's Psychic Surgery"* J. Bernard Ricks describes Terte's techniques:

"The first operation that I witnessed in San Fabian was surgery to remove what was described as a blood clot in

* *The Strange and the Unknown*, Paperback Library, Inc., New York, 1965.

113

the noncirculatory part of the heart. The patient was a middle-aged male, a United States citizen. He is still an active and prominent California businessman. I am not at liberty to reveal his name." The doctors in the States had advised an operation to correct his condition, but he had preferred to take his chances with psychic surgery, Ricks says.

"The operation took place in a hut not different from the others that line the road into the village of four hundred souls. The patient was placed on a simple table and a small group of women gathered at the patient's feet."

Some of these women were also mediums. Their presence was said to enhance the surgeon's power. Hymns were sung and then Brother Terte took his place on the right side of the operating table. Ricks stood opposite him. The Lord's Prayer was recited, then Brother Terte held out his arms "with his fingers pointed straight at the patient's chest and suddenly as if in response to an unseen signal, his arms dropped and he began to massage the patient's chest in the area of the heart. The massage was only a gentle kneading, performed with just the tips of the fingers.

"Within ten seconds after Brother Terte's fingers touched the patient's chest I could see a small black object coming right up through the man's chest—it was a blood clot!" says Ricks. "There was no opening in the chest, but the clot came up and fell right out into Terte's hands. The clot was about the size of my thumbnail and was very bloody, but there was no blood on the patient's body."

Ricks also described an appendectomy and a gall-bladder operation that he saw. Lest the reader think, as I did at

114

first, that this alleged doctor was only palming an object and pretending it came from the patient's body, Ricks described an operation to correct a complaint of colitis. In this an incision was made in the patient's back. "Terte began pulling out long strips of diseased flesh which he deposited in a jar held by Tolentino. The scent of decay was terrible. I saw all of this from a distance of no more than seven or eight inches."

Terte's psychic operations are conducted as services of the Union Espiritista Christiana de Filipinas, a sect which now claims more than five hundred centers and millions of members in the island republic. Union members believe that their Spiritualism is a way of life and not a religion, thus they continue to claim membership in the Roman Catholic church. Terte must travel often to Manila and the other major cities of the Islands. He has taught his techniques to at least twenty others and he is interested in helping still others to master his art. There are efforts being made to bring him to the United States.

Henry Belk has told me personally about his enthusiasm over these psychic surgeons. His recent trip to the Philippines is written up in detail in *The Psychic News*, August 14, 1965, telling about the man Belk most recently investigated: Antonio (Tony) Agpaos, of Quezon City, whom he visited in June, 1965.

Tony is different from the other psychic surgeons we have discussed in that he charges a fee. It is small, however, so that he takes in only about $100 a week. He also has an intelligence above that of the average Filipino, according to Belk. He has travelled around the world and used his healing powers when he visited India.

Henry Belk writes: "I observed his operations on a

great number of people from different cities. I talked to his cousin, Alfredo Cruz, Jr., two years older than Tony, who was brought up with him. I also talked to his attorney friend, Samuel Gines, to a detective, and to Tony's wife, who is about twenty." They have a two-year-old son.

Tony performs from ten to twenty operations per day. He does not advertize. People come to him by word of mouth, and, although Tony is a kind, spiritually evolved person, he has had to move several times to get away from the hordes of people who seek him out. Belk says: "Tony told me that the most operations that he has done in one day was three hundred and seventeen, starting early in the morning and going on into the night."

Henry Belk described an operation that he had personally witnessed, performed on a woman who had a tumor in the abdomen. Tony began to knead her flesh as though he were mixing dough. Then blood began to come out, although he had no knife and had made no incision. An opening appeared which was large enough for him to reach into, and this he did, lifting out the tumor without in any way cutting it free. He handed the tumor to a bystander and then repeated his former kneading process on the abdomen. Instantly the wound was healed.

Having witnessed such an operation, says Belk, you think you have been dreaming. To prove you haven't, there is the extracted tumor before you.

It does not seem to be claimed that Tony Agpaoa's operations are performed under the possession of a spirit surgeon, as Terte's and Arigo's are said to be done. Instead, Tony says he has a spirit helper who is always present during the operations, but he has been instructed not to talk too much about him.

116

The story of how Tony's healing mission began is interesting. It all started in a rice field. A man fell and accidentally stabbed himself in the abdomen. Tony felt a compulsion to put his hand on the wound and it was "miraculously restored and the hole disappeared," says Belk. He soon put his gift to use, and during his entire healing ministry he has never had a fatality.

It would be interesting, and much more conclusive, if we had access to the vital statistics of the communities in which these psychic surgeons operate, would it not? Belk is aware of this, and he is endeavoring to bring some of these healers to this country, just so that they can be observed under conditions which will allow for follow-up case histories and all other controls.

Unfortunately, getting them here is just as difficult as finding mediums who can produce phenomena in the light and flying saucers that will stay around long enough to have their pictures taken. Until then we have only the testimony of eyewitnesses to substantiate the claims.

Debunking the testimony of witnesses by saying they were deluded or hallucinating or showing poor powers of observation is getting pretty trite. It's been done to death, for my money. Poor observation is only claimed for such individuals, you will notice, when they are describing happenings beyond the ordinary. In a court of law Henry Belk's or Puharich's or Sir William Crookes's or Lord Adare's testimony would be considered perfectly valid about a car accident or a petty theft or any other commonplace legal matter. Why should it not be valid, then, when they are testifying about something that most people don't believe could happen? Half the things going on in

117

our present civilization were considered impossible just a few generations ago.

So I'll end with my pet plea for wider mental vision. Let's not close our thoughts to the mysteries allegedly going on in the world. Some of them may be truer than we think.

A Glossary of Supernatural Terms

APPORTS—objects which materialize in the presence of a physical medium. These objects may be the familiar horns, tambourines, and whistles or such sundry articles as flowers, coins, jewelry, and occasional live animals.

AKASHIC RECORDS—supposed cosmic records in which all human deeds, thoughts, and events are recorded. A comprehensive spiritual record, very much like the "Book of Life," which may be consulted by those of the proper spiritual preparation. Conflicting definitions argue that the Akashic Records may or may not be consulted to reveal future events.

ASTRAL BODY—a spiritual essence and intelligence allegedly present in all human beings which, in some people under some conditions, may divorce itself from the physical body for prolonged flights and visits to other locations. Reports of involuntary astral flights are also available. See *The Enigma of Out-of-Body Travel* by Susy Smith.

ALCHEMY—a "science" eagerly studied and pursued by medieval chemists who hoped to convert base elements into silver or gold.

ASTROLOGY—A study of the effects of star and planetary positions on human lives and personalities; also on the behavior of physical elements. See *An Astrology Primer For the Millions* by Carl Payne Tobey, Sherbourne Press, Los Angeles, Calif., 1966.

AUTOMATIC WRITING—a technique by which one relinquishes his own direction of a pen or pencil he is holding, or places his hand lightly on a ouija board, and does not consciously produce the material which is written. Psychologists are inclined to believe that the material invariably comes from the subconscious mind of the sitter. Parapsychologists have a few instances to cite in which information or style of writing has been received of which the sitter was probably incapable. Spiritualists believe that spirit entities produce this material, and warn of the danger that earthbound spirits may take over the writing.

BLACK MASS—the ceremony at which sorcerers and witches are said to have communion with the devil.

CLAIRAUDIENCE—the ability to hear spiritual voices, noises, or other activity inaudible to the human ear.

CLAIRVOYANCE—the ability to see persons and events beyond the recognized limit of human abilities or senses. This phenomena is divided into three basic categories: retrocognition, the ability to see or experience past events; precognition, the faculty to "experience" events that have not yet taken place; and the ability to see instant events which take place at some great distance from the beholder. In every case, the test of true clairvoyance is that it provides the subject with information he could not possibly have derived from any other source or sense. It may occur as a hunch, dream, or impulse as well as in a trance-induced state.

CONTROL—the supernatural agent who acts as a go-between for spirits attempting to communicate through an entranced medium. Referred to by the author as a "master of ceremonies" to the spirit world.

DOWSERS—individuals who are able to "sense" the presence of water below the earth or in unaccessible places. Such individuals often perform their feats with a dowsing rod, generally the branch of a tree. They rely on an extension of the senses rather than any mechanical or electronics devices and are often referred to as water witches.

ECTOPLASM—a substance which is produced from the body of a physical medium who has entered the trance state and is used for materializations. It has been analyzed by one researcher as "colorless, slightly cloudy . . . no smell . . . traces of sputum . . . numerous skin discs . . . numerous granules of the mucus membrane . . . numerous particles of flesh." Often, this ectoplasm takes on a sausage-like shape but it has, on occasion, reportedly taken on shapes which gave it human characteristics.

ESP—Extrasensory perception, the ability to exercise the senses of sight, smell, touch, hearing, or intuition beyond the accepted human boundaries.

FIRE HANDLERS—individuals who are able to handle fire or burning objects with no apparent pain or physical reactions. Many fire handlers are also able to walk on flaming beds of coals. Favored explanations are religious faith and hypnotic trance or post-hypnotic suggestion.

GHOST—an apparition or manifestation of the spirit after bodily death of the individual. The term is a general one, seemingly on its way to obsolescence in favor of the

121

more specific poltergeist, incubus, and succubus, all of which see.

HALLUCINATION—a false sensory stimulus which may cause the individual to believe he has seen, heard, felt, or tasted something which has no reality. The most common hallucinations are visual and auditory.

HOROSCOPE—a picture or map of the heavens, particularly detailing the relative positions of the sun, earth, and other planets at any given time or date. The most common horoscopes are those cast with the birthdate of an individual, country, or organization as the point of reference in time.

INCUBUS—a demon, specifically male in characteristics, who causes nightmares or who may attempt sexual relations with sleeping women.

KARMA—a Sanskrit word meaning action and translated as having the additional meaning of the action of Fate. An essential factor in the religions and philosophies which accept the theory of reincarnation, karma is regarded as the sum total of a person's actions in his past existences. Often, such temporary hardships as losses, setbacks, and disappointments are linked with permanent afflictions such as physical disabilities and classified as karmic debts which must be "worked off" in the individual's present life.

MEDIUM—an individual who receives messages, impressions, and other communications from the Spirit World. Mediumship is divided into two general headings, mental and physical. The mental medium operates without necessarily entering the trance state. He may receive impressions or clairvoyant visions or automatic writings. The physical medium generally operates from a trance state and may produce materializations or apports.

OUIJA BOARD—a name derived from the French "oui" and the German "ja," both words for yes. The ouija board is approximately 2 by 3 feet or some comfortable proportion. It contains the letters of the alphabet, numbers, and some punctuation marks. More sophisticated boards may have the words YES—NO—MAYBE—HELLO—GOOD-BYE printed on them. A pointed indicator called a "planchette" is guided by spiritual forces, spelling out messages. The ouija board is generally placed on a table or flat surface and the planchette physically operated by at least two persons, who rest their fingertips on it.

PARAPSYCHOLOGY—the study of extrasensory perception and phenomena not readily explainable by scientific data.

POLTERGEIST—the word by definition means "noisy ghost." It is given to the type of phenomenon in which sudden disturbances, such as, flying dishes, loud rappings, and overturned furniture, occur. Some researchers believe it is caused by the psychokinetic force in a pubescent child or a person under great tension. Spiritualists believe it is an actual ghost throwing things.

PSYCHIC—sensitive to extrasensory or supernatural phenomena. Or, an individual who is a spiritualistic medium.

PSYCHOKINESIS—ESP's "twin sister." Mind over matter. The suggested power that the mind has over inanimate objects.

REINCARNATION—a belief in a progressive system

123

of spiritual life, after bodily death. The goal is a spiritual enlightenment and improvement until an encompassing communion with the supreme being is achieved, usually understood to mean repeated lives on earth.

SEANCE—a gathering of persons seeking communication with the spirit world, generally involving a medium or mediator through whom contact is made.

SENSITIVE—readily adept at spiritual communication, possessing a high degree of proficiency in ESP ability.

SUCCUBUS—a female demon who plagues the dreams of mortal males and will often have sexual intercourse with her victim.

TRANCE—a state of intense concentration in which the mind is virtually "blanked" of all conscious thought, thus opening it as a telephone or medium of communication from the spirit world.

U.F.O.—Unidentified Flying Objects, the name given to flying saucers and other spacecraft supposedly of an alien world origin. Reported sightings of such flying objects have been recorded throughout ancient and modern histories.

WARLOCK—a wizard, sorcerer, or male witch.

WITCH—a woman who practices either white (good) or black (bad) magic and, therefore, is dedicated to maximum service of either a good or bad end. Also a female sorceress or enchantress.

WITCH DOCTOR—an individual who is able to cure illnesses, cast spells, and, in general, exercise supernatural control over people and elements. Such persons who practice their craft for the good of humanity are often called spirit doctors or spirit healers.

124

Bibliography

Adams, Evangeline, *Astrology, Your Place in the Sun*, Dodd, Mead & Co., New York, 1956.

Barbanell, Maurice, *This Is Spiritualism*, Herbert Jenkins, London, 1959.

Barrett, Sir William F., *On the Threshold of the Unseen*, E. P. Dutton, New York, 1918.

Carrington, Hereward, *The Invisible World*, The Beechhurst Press, New York, 1946.

Court-Treatt, Major C., "Duel by Witchcraft" as told to Helen R. Hunger, *True Stories of the Strange and the Unknown*, Paperback Library, New York, 1965.

DeCamp, L. Sprague and Catherine C., *Spirits, Stars and Spells*, Canaveral Press, New York, 1966.

Dunraven, the Earl of, *Experiences in Spiritualism with D. D. Home*, The F. W. Faxon Co., Boston.

Edwards, Harry, *The Mediumship of Jack Webber*, Rider, London, 1940.

Frazer, James, *The Golden Bough*, Macmillan, London.

Lee, Dal, "Astrology; Facts and Fallacies," *Tomorrow* Magazine, Summer, 1960, Vol. 8, No. 3.

Lorenzen, Coral E., "Did a UFO Land in Florida?" *Fate*

Magazine, October, 1965, Vol. 18, No. 10.

———"Scientists Photograph UFO's in Antarctica," *Fate Magazine*, December, 1965, Vol. 18, No. 12.

Miller, DeWitt, *Reincarnation, the Whole Startling Story*, Bantam Books, New York, 1956.

Oudemans, A. C., *The Great Sea Serpent*, 1892.

Psychic News, London, August 14, 1965.

Richet, Charles, *Thirty Years of Psychical Research*, Macmillan, New York, 1923.

Ricks, J. Bernard, "I Witnessed Terte's Psychic Surgery," *True Stories of The Strange and the Unknown*, Paperback Library, New York, 1965.

Righter, Carroll, *Astrology and You*, Fleet Publishing Corp., 1956.

Rosher, Grace, *Beyond the Horizon*, James Clarke & Co., London, 1961.

Sanderson, Ivan, *Abominable Snowman: Legend Come to Life*, Chilton Co., Philadelphia, 1961.

Smith, Susy, *The Mediumship of Mrs. Leonard*, University Books, New Hyde Park, N.Y., 1963.

———*World of the Strange*, Pyramid Publications, New York, 1963.

Thomas, C. Drayton, *Some New Evidence for Human Survival*, London, W. Collins Sons, 1922.

Two Worlds, November, 1965, No. 3862.

Vallee, Jacques, *Anatomy of a Phenomenon*, Henry Regnery Co., Chicago, 1965.

Wickland, Carl, *Thirty Years among the Dead*, Los Angeles, National Psychological Institute, Inc., 1924.

World Book Encyclopedia Year Book, 1962, Field Enterprises Educational Corp., Chicago, 1962.

5935